Classics

HUNSLET

RUGBY LEAGUE FOOTBALL CLUB

Classics

HUNSLET

RUGBY LEAGUE FOOTBALL CLUB

PHIL HODGSON

TEMPUS

*In homage to the many men and women who have served the
Hunslet club so well for the past century-and-a-quarter.*

First published 2006

Tempus Publishing Limited
The Mill, Brimscombe Port,
Stroud, Gloucestershire, GL5 2QG
www.tempus-publishing.com

British Library Cataloguing in Publication Data.
A catalogue record for this book is available from the British Library.

ISBN 0 7524 3709 7

Typesetting and origination by Tempus Publishing Limited.
Printed in Great Britain.

Acknowledgements

It would not be possible to compile what amounts to an historical review of any club without the help, directly and indirectly, of a legion of people. Given the fact that Hunslet's greatest days were almost a century ago many of those folk will now be long gone, but the contributions of the likes of Flaneur of the *Leeds Mercury*, who was lucky enough to report on the deeds of Albert Goldthorpe and the Terrible Six in achieving All Four Cups glory, cannot be understated. In the more modern era, I am grateful in particular to Harry Jepson, the long-serving secretary when Hunslet were last a major force, for his unstinting help and advice, while the Rugby Football League's historian Tony Collins, Robert Gate and the ever-patient Michael Turner, Graham Morris, Len Garbett, Denis Whittle and Mike Sterriker have never hesitated (despite what must have seemed at times to be interminable requests for more information) to supply extra detail.

I doubt whether I could have completed this account without the vast amount of statistical data painstakingly and accurately compiled by Steve Calline. Raymond Fletcher and Irving Saxton, both historians of the highest order, have also provided with their work over many years detail that has contributed to the spine of this book.

I am indebted to Les Hoole, Paul Butterfield, Dave Williams, Graham Brown at the *Huddersfield Examiner* and, as ever, Jayne Marsden at the *Yorkshire Post* Library for the loan or release of so many superb photographs and sketches, and I am also grateful to Tim Butcher of the *Rugby Leaguer* and *League Express* for readily granting permission to reproduce articles from my days with the *Leaguer*.

All the staff at Leeds Reference Library (another long-suffering bunch) have been unfailingly supportive despite countless hours of pestering, as have their colleagues in Wakefield, while Holly Bennion, of Tempus Publishing, has been the ultimate professional and valiantly – very valiantly – patient, a trait shared, yet again, by my ever-supportive wife Julia and our children Sam, Jack and Sarah.

This book would not, however, have been possible without the many fine players who have served the club, in its various manifestations, for the past 122 years and I am delighted that one of the best of those, Ginger Burnell, agreed to contribute a foreword that, typically, came from the heart. My heartfelt thanks, for their help in a myriad of ways, also go to Phil Caplan, Gina Coldrick, Brian Colley, A.L. Drewry, Stuart Duffy, Heather Dunkerley (*Oldham Evening Chronicle*), David Elliott, Sean Fagan (RL1908.com), Ray French, Gary Halloway, Roger Halstead, Patricia Hodgson, Trevor Hunt, John Huxley, Ian Johnson, Scott Johnson, John Kear, *League Weekly*, John Ledger (*Yorkshire Post*), Stan Lewandowski, Raymond Lister, Graham Lovett, Alan Metcalfe, Sheila Metcalfe, David Middleton (League Information Services), Roger Millward, Geoffrey Moorhouse, Keith Nutter, Maurice Oldroyd, Bob Pickles, Bill Ramsey, Keith Rayson, Michael Rhodes, Chris Roberts (*Huddersfield Examiner*), Diane Rogerson, Syd Rooke, Mike Rylance, Harry Sheard, Stuart Sheard, David Smart, Bryan Smith, Peter Smith (*Yorkshire Evening Post*), Stewart Smith, David Spence, Alan Stephenson, 'Stix' (Leeds United), Ken Sykes, Denis Tate, Lesley Temlett, Vanessa Toulmin, Karl Waddicor, Frank Watson, Trevor Watson and Donna Williams. Finally, I owe a huge debt to my old friend Graham Lister. It's very unlikely that I would have written this book, or indeed spent much of the last four decades involved in various ways with the greatest sport of all, but for a chance combination of circumstances one Saturday afternoon in the autumn of 1963.

Foreword

Playing for Hunslet was a boyhood dream for most lads who, like me, were brought up in south Leeds, and I had no doubts at all in 1941 about signing for the club. I wasn't alone. There were five or six of us who put pen to paper at Parkside at the same time. But because the club, like so many others, was struggling during the Second World War none of us got so much as a halfpenny! Even so, I was very happy to be on Hunslet's books and even happier when I returned from active service.

If I thought being brought up in a family of thirteen was hard, so was four years in a submarine, and after that I was only too glad to return to dry land and resume my career with Hunslet. They were great days as, I'm sure, the men who had played for the club before me would have agreed and as, I'm equally sure, those who have followed will attest about their own eras.

Not that the club's management always made life easy. The Hunslet committee was noted for watching its purse strings – I suppose that was one way of keeping the club afloat – and when a pair of boots provided by Clarks on Waterloo Road split I spent the next five or six years wearing a pair that were one-and-a-half sizes too big! I wore those boots while playing for Hunslet, Yorkshire and Great Britain and I only got around the size problem by wearing two pairs of socks. The second pair were cut short and I had to wrap white tape around them and the boots to keep everything in place. It didn't help that my teammates took the mickey and said I was trying to look fancy, but that was part of the team spirit and the ethos of the club.

I never really thought of playing for anybody else, despite very good offers by St Helens, Leeds and Huddersfield, and I'm sure most of the other players felt the same way. We were a match for any other side in the league, and a lot of that was due to the fact that the team was made up mainly of local lads. It was an honour to play for Hunslet and we would give our hearts to win. The community around us also cared – passionately – and we were left in no doubt in the pubs and clubs of south Leeds, or at work, if we'd had a bad game. Old women weren't slow either to shout 'you useless so-and-so, Burnell' at me across the street if they thought I hadn't performed!

But that's all part of people caring about this wonderful club and I'm delighted to have been asked to provide the foreword for this book. Hunslet have been involved in many great games, some of them the best in rugby league's history, and I'm sure the club's own supporters and those of other teams will enjoy reminiscing about those matches.

Alf 'Ginger' Burnell
Hunslet RLFC 1946-1958
December 2005

Introduction

We like to think that we are in control of our own destinies, that we choose the road down which our respective lives progress, and that we can be selective over the various diversions that crop up from time to time. The reality is rather different, most notably in terms of affairs of the heart.

Apart from those liaisons more usually catered for by Mills and Boon, it's arguable that no purer love exists than that held by a man for the football club to which he became attached as a child. The lifelong love for a particular woman, which admittedly can run a reasonably close second, depends initially on the roulette wheel of romance settling on a meeting in the first place; and it's no different in respect of the bond that so many of us, whichever team we support, have with an entity often described disparagingly as 'that bloody lot' or worse.

So it was that my own love affair with Hunslet – and, on a wider basis, with the sport of rugby league – began through pure chance one autumn afternoon in 1963. I owe my old mate Graham Lister and his late dad, Ray, a great debt for hanging about for me after I'd called out of the blue that Saturday with the intention of 'playing out'. 'Lisa' was, instead, going down to Parkside and was about to climb into the back of his dad's van. Ray, not a man to mince words – a handy attribute in his part-time job at Jeff Stevenson's pub, the Anchor – simply told me: 'Run back home for the tanner entry charge and you can come with us.' After a quick sprint back to my mam, and a slower jog back, I was on my way to watch Hunslet for the first time, totally unaware that my entire life would take a different route from that day on. I was hooked. I've supported the south Leeds club ever since – even working on the scoreboard at Mother Benson's End with mates like Lisa, Dave (Spanner) Spence, Steve Price, Steve Vernon and my cousin Mick when the first kids to turn up on matchday did the job – and played for their Under-17s side in the late 1960s.

Like a junkie caught in an ever-downward spiral, I eventually became so embroiled in the sport that I've now spent over a decade as a rugby league journalist. This is largely due to ('the fault of' might be a better phrase!) Hunslet who, despite losing that fateful day in 1963 to Hull KR, were a power at the time. I was perhaps fortunate to 'discover' them when they were a match for any team in the land. The memories of what, now I come to think about it, were only a couple of years at most of being a top-ranking outfit since I became a supporter have helped sustain me through what in truth has been a testing ensuing forty years for a team that was once unarguably the best in the country and had on board every available trophy to prove it. I still remember the magical moment when, as an eleven-year-old, I stumbled on a photograph of the great Albert Goldthorpe with all four cups' in the old 'Green Final' and learned, with pride fit to burst, that Hunslet – my Hunslet – had been the first of only three clubs to pull off that unimaginable feat.

There were successes, of a sort, to follow in my childhood, not least the appearance at Wembley in 1965 when my overnight tears at what, to me, was an unexpected defeat turned to tears of joy the following morning when the Sunday papers explained that the Parksiders, despite losing to Wigan, were actually winners because of the wonderful part they had played in the greatest of finals. It was more painful a few months later when my favourites lost to rank outsiders Bradford Northern in the Yorkshire Cup final and that proved to be Hunslet's last appearance on the major stage as the club was allowed to drift.

Parkside was sold less than eight years later (when Spanner and I went down to the ground and 'rescued' a couple of letters off the scoreboard) and Hunslet, despite one or two bright periods, have never been able to recover their former pre-eminence. The saving grace is that it's actually much harder supporting a team that's expected to win trophies, leading to almost inevitable disappointment, than following a side with little hope of success. That's why I took particular pleasure in writing the story of Hunslet's magnificent victory over mighty Hull KR in the Challenge Cup in 1983, a win engineered by veteran loose forward Johnny Wolford – who remains possibly the best player I've ever seen – that I hadn't thought possible beforehand. My wife Julia, sadly sucked into the Hunslet fever after meeting me, rightly had more faith than I had in the men who played in that wonderful game. They, and those who beat Super League's Huddersfield in the same competition in 2003, exemplify the old Parkside spirit that served the club so well from 1888 to 1973.

It's a spirit that helped Geoff Gunney, Gordon Murray and others launch New Hunslet in 1973 when all seemed lost following the sale of Parkside. And it's a spirit that has kept the current bearers of the tradition, the Hawks, alive through the tireless efforts of the former chairman Grahame Liles and his wife Margaret, and long-serving directors Shaun Cluderay and Paul Mallinson. They have been followed by present chairman Ian Johnson, whose task – like theirs – has been made all the harder by the decision of the Rugby Football League not to grant Hunslet promotion to Super League in 1999.

I hope, in this book, to have captured the many highs and, admittedly, some of the lows of a great club, one that is invoked by folk all around the globe as the club they support – and an entity, through its several guises, that certainly enjoys the goodwill of people throughout the wider rugby league community. Sadly, many of the major matches featured are now from an age long gone, including the period prior to the Great Split of 1895 when Hunslet was a successful rugby union club, and the Northern Union era when the Parksiders were the team to beat; a task that proved to be near-impossible for most opponents.

The fact remains, however, that south Leeds is, as it always has been, a hotbed of rugby league talent. My hope is that this book may go some way to reminding youngsters in the area of the fine legacy left by their predecessors, and that the tradition of signing for Hunslet in preference to any other club can and should be revived. If that happens Hunslet, rest assured, will once again become a major power.

Phil Hodgson
December 2005

Postscript: The emotive power of Parkside was again brought home to me on Christmas Day 2005 when I opened a present from Spanner. It was the 'G' he had retrieved from the scoreboard at Mother Benson's End that bleak day in 1973, which is now reunited with the 'A' that has been in my care for over thirty-two years. Thanks, Span. No gift could mean more.

Classic Matches

14 March 1885	Leeds St Johns
11 February 1888	Mirfield
23 April 1892	Leeds
7 September 1895	Warrington
30 April 1898	Bradford
29 April 1899	Oldham
7 March 1903	Leeds
2 December 1905	Halifax
21 December 1907	Halifax
26 December 1907	New Zealand
29 February 1908	Leeds
14 March 1908	Oldham
28 March 1908	Barrow
11 April 1908	Broughton Rangers
18 April 1908	Broughton Rangers
25 April 1908	Hull
2 May 1908	Oldham
9 May 1908	Oldham
13 March 1909	Leeds
30 November 1929	Hull Kingston Rovers
25 December 1929	Australia
5 May 1934	Widnes
23 April 1938	Barrow
30 April 1938	Leeds
16 March 1946	Salford
30 March 1946	Wakefield Trinity
20 March 1954	Huddersfield
2 May 1959	Wigan
16 May 1959	St Helens
27 October 1962	Hull Kingston Rovers
12 February 1964	Wakefield Trinity
6 February 1965	Oldham
13 March 1965	Leeds
10 April 1965	Wakefield Trinity
8 May 1965	Wigan
27 September 1965	Castleford
16 October 1965	Bradford Northern
21 April 1973	York
26 August 1973	Huyton
23 October 1974	Widnes
13 February 1983	Hull Kingston Rovers
13 March 1983	Castleford
27 February 1985	Leigh
14 April 1985	Wigan
17 May 1887	Swinton
12 February 1995	Salford
19 November 1995	Leigh Centurions
23 July 1997	Widnes Vikings
25 September 1999	Dewsbury Rams
9 February 2003	Huddersfield Giants

HUNSLET v. LEEDS ST JOHNS

Date: 14 March 1885
Location: Woodhouse Hill

Yorkshire Challenge Cup
Referee: Mr Whitehead (Wakefield)

Hunslet, in only their second season, made the rest of the rugby world and the wider sporting public sit up and take notice with a victory over an established power in the famous Yorkshire Rugby Union Cup, also affectionately known as 'T'owd tin pot'. The fledgling club had no right to anticipate victory but the fact that 7,000, including the Lord Mayor of Leeds, turned up for the game suggests that not only those within the home camp believed that a major upset against the forerunners of Leeds RLFC and Leeds Rhinos was on the cards. Hunslet had to contend too with one counter-attraction being held in the city that day, while up in London a meeting was being held at the Mansion House charged with raising funds for a memorial to General Gordon of Khartoum. The event nearer home, at the Leeds Philosophical Hall, was of the Navvy Mission Society although how many potential rugby fans would have been diverted is open to question, the *Yorkshire Post* reporting that the large audience included, 'many ladies connected with various philanthropic movements in the town and neighbourhood.'

Woodhouse Hill was also packed to the seams as Hunslet sought to add St Johns to the scalps of Elland and Bingley. Elland had been beaten by 2 goals and 6 minors to a goal and 4 minors before a 2,000 home crowd, while Bingley had been disposed of, also at home, to the tune of 1 goal, 1 try and 9 minors to 6 minors at the second round stage. That 2,000 gate, incidentally, emulated the attendance for the visit to Holbeck on 18 October as confirmation of the growing interest in rugby south of the river. Holbeck were to join the Northern Union in its second season, 1896/97, only to switch to soccer as Leeds City years later after losing a play-off with St Helens to determine promotion from Division Two. City were subsequently thrown out of the Football League in 1919 for irregular payments to players and were immediately replaced by Leeds United.

Hunslet, who had survived an appeal by Bingley that North had been ineligible, won as thrilling a match as has ever taken place between the two great clubs by virtue of a try for Patchett in extra time after a scoreless eighty minutes. The *Yorkshire Post* reported: 'The game proved a very close one, the younger organisation, after an extended period of play, proving victorious by a try. Every credit is due to the Hunslet men for the plucky front they showed their better-known opponents and their victory was very popular among the large body of local supporters present. The winning forwards played a strong, tireless game and were as fresh at the finish as at the beginning; and the half backs were as active as eels, Patchett especially doing a lot of work and securing the winning try in capital style.' The *Post* scribe paid tribute to Carr in the Hunslet three-quarters, with Gilston also said to be highly effective, doing 'some smart things at times'. St Johns, by contrast, were 'most disappointing to their friends. Their forwards were beaten in the packs, they lacked combination and their following up and tackling were bad. Had there been any combination at all two tries must have resulted in the second half of the game, but through a want of a little head work the opportunities

---

Hunslet 1 try, 6 minors   **Leeds St Johns 5 minors**

(after extra time)

William 'Billy' Gilston, a shining light in the early days of the Hunslet club.

were lost and Hunslet snatched an unexpected victory. Potter, as usual, was the mainstay of the (Leeds) backs; but, with the exception of Burrell, the other backs were very disappointing, Hirst's exhibition being miserable in the extreme.'

The sensational victory helped propel Hunslet to the forefront of the sporting world and ensured that rugby held sway over the Association code in south Leeds for many years. Players of note were attracted to the club and perhaps the only individual with reservations over the success was the club's cobbler, Clark's of Waterloo Road. Mr Clark, charged with the task of repairing the players' boots before the match, had been asked for a quote and reportedly answered, '6d a pair if you lose, but nowt if you win.' A costly response but Mr Clark perhaps joined in the general celebrations in Hunslet pubs that night, when the pints flowed freely and whisky was said to have been served in pots.

Hunslet went on to meet mighty Bradford, one of the oldest clubs in the game and the current holders of 'T'owd tin pot', in the next round. It was a hurdle too far for the fledgling club that, before an 8,000 crowd, crashed out of the competition by 7 goals, 6 tries and 10 minors to 1 minor. But a marker had, without doubt, been set by the display against Leeds St Johns; a marker that would pave the way for Yorkshire Cup success seven years later and even greater achievements over the ensuing decades. It was a remarkable change of fortune for the club that, at Christmas, had struggled to raise a team and had only decided to continue after one player, Sam Wood, saw a hare and declared it a 'lucky omen.'

Hunslet: Hoole, Carr, North, Gilston, Ellis, Patchett, Garland, Gilbert, Groves, Harrison, Henderson, Scott, E. Thackeray, Tomlinson, Wreath.

Leeds St Johns: Peacock, Hirst, Crosfield, Cockrell, Potter, Burrell, Moore, Annal, TP Peacock, Sharp, Eddison, Smith, Watson, Shaw, Glover.

Hunslet v. Mirfield

Date: 11 February 1888   Friendly

Location: Parkside

There was relatively little fanfare as Hunslet moved into their new home at Parkside with a low-key fixture with Mirfield. The official opening was planned for the game with Brighouse Rangers fourteen days later, with the opening ceremony to be performed by the Mayor of Leeds, Alderman A. Scarr. Nevertheless, there were due celebrations for the visit of Mirfield. The *Yorkshire Post*, previewing the weekend's local rugby union matches, ventured: 'Hunslet, whose forwards are a really accomplished set of players, open their new ground at Parkside with a game against Mirfield, a band being in attendance. In this case there is only one opinion about the result, and that is that the home men should prove the victors of an exciting match.'

Other than the reference to the band, there was little hint that the first tentative step was being taken on an adventure that would run for eighty-five years, only ending with the club's sad demise in 1973. Nevertheless, a healthy crowd turned up for the contest, the *Yorkshire Post* revealing that the game was, 'played on the Park Side [*sic*] Ground, Hunslet, in the presence of about 5,000 spectators.' The south Leeds throng were treated to a match that Hunslet won convincingly enough, with the tone set from the beginning. Captain Billy Gilston had the honour of being the first man to put hand or boot to ball at Parkside, his kick-off finding touch in the Mirfield 25 and Stoddart going close with a drop goal attempt from the attacking position. Hunslet centre Greenwood 'gained further ground by a judicious drop' with Mirfield's Barraclough sending the ball back to midfield and home stand-off Jones responding in kind with a 'neat screw kick'. Greenwood, latching onto a pass by Stoddart, made good ground with a clever dodgy run, forcing Mirfield three-quarter Milner to 'make a mark' but his relieving kick counted for little. Jones, having an influential kicking game, put the visitors under further pressure with a 'grand drop', which took play to the Mirfield line where 'hot scrimmaging ensued'.

As half-time approached, a Mirfield clearing kick led to Matt Carr making a mark for the Parksiders, and scrum half Lonsdale broke to the visitors' 25 to set up the position from which Milner was forced to touch down behind his own try line and concede a minor point. Mirfield, however, responded in kind as the second half opened, Barraclough registering a dead ball with a huge punt and fellow three-quarter Dyson forcing a minor point with a fine run to the Hunslet 25 from the drop out.

Hunslet, though, quickly retrieved the advantage, Greenwood racing through and Stoddart continuing the attack to gain a minor point. The home side's pressure remained relentless, Mirfield's drop out following the minor point securing short-lived position in the Hunslet 25 but Summerhill and Gilston, with several teammates, responded with a good dribble.

With play settling into a midfield war of attrition, it fell to the Hunslet pack to break away to the Mirfield line and force another minor point. From the resultant drop out Jones attacked, Dyson also threatening, only to be 'held before he could get away'. A drop goal attempt by Jones was

Hunslet 1 try, 6 minors   **Mirfield 2 minors**

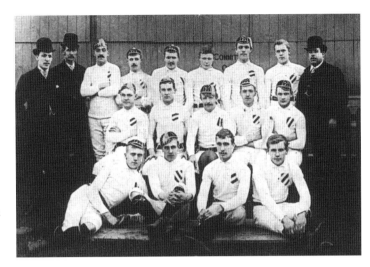

The Hunslet side that met Mirfield's near neighbours Dewsbury at Parkside in November 1889. From left to right, back row: T. Groves, T. Crook, J. Skirrow, M. Carr, E. Kaye, W. Goldthorpe, I. Summerhill, J. Goldthorpe, G. Williamson. Middle row: T. Stevens, J. Carroll, W.H. Gilston, J. Rathmell, J. Mosley. Front row: W. Stephens, W. Townsend, C. Lapping, A.E. Goldthorpe.

unsuccessful, a minor resulting, and Carr kept up the pressure from the drop out with an astute. The mauled Mirfield side, however, were unable to repel Hunslet for much longer. With time running out Carr 'picked up at the Mirfield 25 and, defying all opposition, got over the line'. The conversion attempt failed but, as the referee blew for time, Hunslet had won their first game at their new ground by 1 try and 6 minors to 2 minors.

Hunslet played four more matches at their new home before the end of the season. Brighouse Rangers travelled to Parkside fourteen days later for a Yorkshire Cup first round match and eased to the second round stage with 1 goal and 1 minor to Hunslet's 2 tries and 1 minor. Manningham were then disposed of by 2 goals and 3 minors to 1 minor before Dewsbury, the next visitors, inflicted defeat on their hosts, scoring 1 goal to Hunslet's try and 4 minors. The campaign, however, ended with two successive victories. Salterhebble were routed by 2 goals, 3 tries and 4 minors to nil, and Hunslet then went on to win at Kirkstall courtesy of 2 goals and 6 minors to a goal and 2 minors. Parkside become something of a citadel and no team, however grand, relished the prospect of meeting Hunslet there. It was also testament to the endeavours of the club's founding fathers. Due tribute was paid in the foreword to the jubilee souvenir programme fifty years later, which stated: 'It has been a working men's club since its formation and is today. The club was founded by working men, and it has been the working men's pride to develop and manage it throughout.

'These few sentences, spoken by one of the founders of the Hunslet Club twenty years after it was formed, still give the keynote of the Club's character, even after twenty years have elapsed. The democratic views of those hardy pioneers of the eighties, who developed the Club in its infancy, still perpetuate and in honouring our Golden Jubilee of 50 years' tenancy at Parkside, we are proud of the fact that the Club still retains its glorious traditions. WELL PLAYED, HUNSLET!'

Hunslet: Broughton, Carr, Greenwood, Stoddart, Jones, Lonsdale, Bennett, Gilston, William Goldthorpe, Groves, Henderson, Mosley, Skirrow, Summerhill, W. White.

Mirfield: Parkinson, Milner, Dyson, Barraclough, Jennings, Day, Atkinson, Brooke, Kaye, Wilson, Whitehead, Greenwood, Laycock, Collins, Norcross.

HUNSLET v. LEEDS

Date: 23 April 1892

Location: Fartown, Huddersfield

Yorkshire Cup final

Referee: Mr Humphreys (Midlands Society)

An attempt by a number of Leeds players to relax in Knaresborough on the eve of one of the most important games in their careers backfired badly. The Leeds men should, with hindsight, have perhaps paid a visit to Mother Shipton's Cave for hints as to what might befall them on the rest of the trip – and during the following day's Yorkshire Cup final – before venturing onto the river.

As the *Yorkshire Post* reported on the morning of the game: 'The football public generally, and especially that portion which is wrapped up in the fortunes of the Leeds men in their struggle at Huddersfield today, were considerably alarmed last evening by a report of a serious disaster which was said to have befallen them at Knaresborough. On investigation, however, the affair proved much less serious than at first supposed. A portion of the team, it appears, left yesterday for Knaresborough, for a day's outing, and one item which found general favour was a tow on the Nidd.

'For this purpose they engaged boats and it appears that Donaldson, who is one of the best forwards in the team, changed from one of the boats into a canoe, in which he got out to midstream. Then the canoe suddenly capsized, and he was precipitated into the river, which at that point is about eight or nine feet deep. The explanation of the accident is that Donaldson, missing his stroke, fell sideways and overbalancing the canoe was thrown into the stream.

'Though the affair is regarded by many as a joke, those who were present hold quite a different view, which is not surprising when it is learnt that it was some seconds before the immersed player came to the surface, he having, as it turned out, caught his foot in something at the bottom.

'When he did come up he made an effort to swim ashore and with the assistance of Mr H. Sewell was safely landed in a condition very much exhausted. He was, in fact, in a complete stupor. Restoratives having been supplied, he was conveyed to the Boar's Head Hotel, where the team was staying. There he was put to bed and, after a few hours, was all right. Lewthwaite, who also got into the water, was rescued with some little difficulty by his comrades. It is not thought that Hudson will be able to play today, in which case Load will probably take his place, and rumour was current last night that there would be another absentee.'

Leeds were duly overwhelmed in a game which the *Yorkshire Post*, in its preview, had reflected: 'Never in our long experience, and we have not missed a final tie since the Cup was instituted, has the day of the struggle arrived and found opinions as to the result so equally divided. For several weeks the contestants have been playing and yet though they have been closely watched and the action of each man on the two sides noted, contrasted and reasoned from, scarcely anyone seems confident as to what will happen.

'This general feeling of uncertainty gives promise of splendid sport for the thousands who will throng the well-appointed and capacious ground of the Huddersfield Club this afternoon, but it by no means follows that the match will be a very close one. The probabilities, however, all point that

Hunslet 21   Leeds 0

The first of many! Hunslet pose proudly with t'owd tin pot – the Yorkshire Cup – in 1892.

way. A great deal has been said about the untrustworthy nature of form in Cup-tie matches, but form has – of late years, at least – been found more trustworthy than the play shown in ordinary club encounters.

'On the face of this form it is impossible – judging from the best match tests – to separate the two teams. So far as consistency goes, Hunslet have had the more successful Cup season, although Leeds have accomplished some wonderful performances, such, for instance, as beating Halifax, who were regarded as the most accomplished team in the competition and likely, with a fair amount of luck, to run into the final round.'

The *Post* summed up: 'He who follows the sport in Leeds on the south side of the Aire may think, because he wishes, that Hunslet will win. Those, on the other hand, who reside on the north side of the river will not easily believe that Leeds can be beaten.'

Those among the 25,000 crowd who hailed from north of the Aire were, in fact, compelled to acknowledge the fallibility of their favourites as Hunslet eased to a comfortable victory under the new scoring system, introduced that season, of 2 points for a try, 3 points for a conversion, 3 points for a penalty and 4 points for a drop goal. The Parksiders, playing in 'white costumes', brought the Yorkshire Cup to the city for the first time, dominating the second period after a scoreless first half in which it appeared that the 'Leeds forwards had met more than their equals, if not their betters.' Young Albert Goldthorpe was only two feet short with an attempted goal from a 'mark' and then unaccountably missed a simple free-kick, Leeds stand off J.R. Potter (heavier than any of the Hunslet forwards, in an odd precursor to the 1938 championship final when Aussie Vic Hey emulated his predecessor) finding touch around halfway with the return. Jack Rathmell's charge

Hunslet v. Leeds

An early action shot. Hunslet qualified for the final with a 12-3 victory over Liversedge at Thrum Hall.

Joe Lewthwaite, who played against Hunslet in the 1892 Yorkshire Cup final, went on to become the chairman of Hunslet. He is caricatured, together with other Parkside personalities, in 1947.

through the opposition's ranks from the throw-in, halted by a tackle on the line – where Leeds experienced a 'rather warm time of it' – suggested that Hunslet were about to take a grip on proceedings. Summergill, however, went close to putting Leeds in front, his drop goal attempt being charged down before full-back Walter Goldthorpe gave Hunslet a lead they were to retain. 'The next notable instance,' reported the *Yorkshire Post*, 'was a clever drop by Walter Goldthorpe which that player followed up so well that he was on Wilkinson before he could gather the ball. This allowed the Hunslet full-back to secure possession and he dashed in under the posts amid a scene rarely witnessed on a football field. Lapping brought the leather out and A. Goldthorpe scored a goal, much to the evident satisfaction of the Hunslet contingent.'

Albert Goldthorpe was wide with another attempted goal from a 'mark' but Rathmell scored a try after charging down a Leeds clearance kick and Albert Goldthorpe also raced over after 'some fine passing occurred between the Hunslet backs. It was started by the halves and in the end Albert Goldthorpe galloped into his stride. He passed first one man and then another and, dodging Summergill cleverly, planted the ball over the line in a favourable position.'

James Goldthorpe, who would later become the secretary at Leeds, went on to score two late tries, one by 'clever dodging' and the other by 'dashing through the Leeds backs and rushing along the terrace side of the ground like a deer. Wilkinson could not bring him down, and a try was scored, the sprinter having covered the whole length of the ground.' Kaye scored next, Albert Goldthorpe closing with three goals, to complete an emphatic win that belied the predictions of a closely fought encounter.

Cumbrian Joe Lewthwaite came close to drowning in the river Nidd when the Leeds team visited Knaresborough on the eve of the final. Lewthwaite later switched to Hunslet, giving the club wonderful service in many capacities for over half a century. He is pictured, as a proud chairman, presenting Hector Crowther with a citation.

Leeds captain Potter said, to a 'somewhat mixed reception' at the post-match presentation, that his club felt they had faced the strongest opposition in Yorkshire. They had thought the match would be 'much nearer' and that the score would not be so large. Undoubtedly, he insisted, on that day's match Hunslet would beat 'not only Leeds but the rest of England.'

Joe Lewthwaite who, with Donaldson, had almost drowned in the river Nidd two days earlier, may have pondered on this more than most. The following season he left Leeds for Hunslet, serving the club wonderfully well as a player, committee man, chairman and then president in a fifty-six-year association that only ended with his death in 1948.

The supporters, too, were suitably enthused. The waiting throng at the Cemetery Tavern on Woodhouse Hill, whiling away the time with tunes of the day such as *Bicycle made for Two*, were quickly taught a Russian war song by one of their number who had been a sailor. Hunslet's players, having travelled from Leeds railway station by wagonnette, were greeted (for the first time but certainly not the last) by the refrain *We've Swept the Seas Before Boys, and So We Shall Again*.

Hunslet: W. Goldthorpe, J. Goldthorpe, A.E. Goldthorpe, Wright, Townsend, Lapping, Bennett, Gilston, Groves, Kaye, Liversedge, Moore, Mosley, Rathmell, Skirrow.

Leeds: Wilkinson, Place, Summersgill, Walker, Potter, Watts, Donaldson, Lorriman, Pickles, Naylor, Fletcher, Cousins, Monroe, Watson, Lewthwaite.

WARRINGTON v. HUNSLET

Date: 7 September 1895   **Northern Union**
Location: Wilderspool   **Referee:** Mr Slevin (Wigan)

Nine days after the historic meeting of member clubs of the Yorkshire Senior Competition and the Lancashire Combination at the George Hotel, Huddersfield, the Northern Union staged its first round of fixtures. Twenty of the twenty-one clubs present at the debate on 29 August 1895 had opted to withdraw from the Rugby Football Union, with Stockport gaining admission upon submitting an application by telegraph. Dewsbury, who had declined to join after their delegate had sought the views of his committee over the proposal that 'the clubs here represented decided to form a Northern Rugby Football Union, and pledge themselves to push forward without delay its establishment on the principle of payment for bona-fide broken-time only,' remained – for the time being – within the Rugby Union, with Runcorn taking their place among the visionaries.

The first results in the Northern Union were: Batley 7, Hull 3; Bradford 11, Wakefield Trinity 0; Broughton Rangers 0, Wigan 9; Leigh 3, Leeds 6; Liversedge 0, Halifax 5; Runcorn 15, Widnes 4; St Helens 8, Rochdale 3; Stockport 0, Brighouse Rangers 5; Tyldesley 6, Manningham 0. Huddersfield and Oldham sat out the epoch-making day, while Hunslet made their mark with a trip across the Pennines to Warrington, who had been formed in 1875, for the remaining game.

The Parksiders, whose ground had been closed by the Rugby Football Union until the first Saturday in December because of crowd trouble following the 3-0 defeat by Brighouse the previous April, travelled with a weakened side because of cricket commitments and the concerns of several players over being professionalised and the consequent very real danger of being unable to take part in cricket, athletics or cycling. Albert Goldthorpe was among the absentees on a balmy late-summer's day, described in one report as 'too genial for keen football', and in another as 'more fit for cricket than football'. Hunslet held sway in the early stages. Warrington, however, weathered the storm – or, more accurately, the oppressive heat – with Joe Boscow thwarting a promising attack by the visitors' three-quarters. Hunslet continued to apply pressure, aided by a couple of penalties, before the Wire assumed territorial advantage through a lengthy dribble by Sankey. Indeed, Warrington came close to scoring first when winger Fair Barber crossed the Hunslet try line, only to be forced into touch in-goal by a hard-working defence in which Walter Goldthorpe was prominent. That was the closest either side came to opening its account in a scoreless first half.

Warrington launched the second period the stronger but the Parksiders replied effectively through Jack Mitchell and Charlie Lapping. Hunslet appeared set for an inaugural victory in the Northern Union when Goldthorpe kicked a drop goal, emulating his brother Albert's renowned abilities as the finest exponent of the craft by taking possession near touch and, after beating several men, fly-kicking the ball over the home crossbar. Victory, however, was to rest with Warrington. The Lancastrians' response was immediate, a rush to the Hunslet goal line resulting in Foden scoring a

---

Warrington 5   Hunslet 4

WARRINGTON v. HUNSLET

Hunslet's first game as a professional rugby club was at Wilderspool and the stadium proved to be an unhappy hunting ground. The Parksiders never managed to win there but came very close in 1963 when, as Division Two underdogs, they were beaten 7-5 in the quarter-finals of the Challenge Cup. Scrum half Jeff Stevenson, assisted by Bill Ramsey, hauls down a Wire man. Brian Gabbitas looks on.

try and Burton kicking a 'splendid' goal from close to the touchline. That was the final incident in a game that Warrington, by common consent, deserved to win.

Ironically, the result set the tone for the next 109 years. From 1895 until Warrington's move to the Halliwell Jones Stadium in 2004, Hunslet were unable to register a single win at Wilderspool. The Parksiders, however, were to enjoy more success in the inaugural campaign. Twenty-four victories and two draws from their forty-two games secured a healthy seventh position in the final table. Warrington, meanwhile, finished below halfway, thirteenth with 17 wins and 5 draws. Brighouse and Bradford both drew 9 of their games, while Runcorn, Tyldesley, St Helens, Stockport, Broughton Rangers and Rochdale Hornets each shared the spoils in 8 fixtures; suggesting generally intense competition certain to delight aficionados of the fledgling code. It was also likely to please Hunslet's supporters who, but for the launch of the Northern Union, could have found themselves deprived of any football at all. The home fixture with Brighouse the previous spring had put the club's future in some jeopardy, with twenty-one policemen being called to Parkside to calm matters after attacks on the match official. Whether or not Hunslet would have survived the seven-month ban from their own home will never be known. The reprieve, in the shape of the Northern Union, allowed their supporters – relieved and now on better behaviour – to continue to enjoy quality rugby and 6,000 turned up at Parkside, many of them no doubt gratefully, seven days after the reverse at Warrington for the home game with Oldham. Hunslet, happily, got off the mark immediately with a 16-8 victory. Attendances remained highly satisfactory, highlighted by a gate of 10,000 for the visit of Leeds on 26 October when honours were even in the 3-3 draw. The Parksiders, though, were unable to gain revenge over Warrington when the Wire crossed the Pennines for the return fixture in mid-February. Warrington carved out a 5-3 interval lead and held on for a hard-earned win in a scoreless second half.

Warrington: Boscow, Barber, O'Brien, Burton, Carey, Foden, Bate, Turner, Dakin, Taylor, Nevins, Berry, Sankey, Swift, Saunders.

Hunslet: W. Goldthorpe, Hannah, Wright, Townsend, Mitchell, Lapping, Gillings, Barraclough, Deacon, Greenwood, Hill, Kaye, Mawson, Rubrey, Walsh.

HUNSLET v. BRADFORD

Date: 30 April 1898

Location: Headingley, Leeds

Yorkshire Senior Competition Championship Play-off

Referee: Mr Farrar (Halifax)

Hunslet had the better of a tight clash with the men from Park Avenue to become the second winners of the Yorkshire Senior Competition in the middle of a five-year period in which the Northern Union opted for regional rather than national competition. The Parksiders had finished top of the table, ahead of Bradford on points difference, with 22 victories and 4 draws from 30 fixtures; their opponents had won 23 games, sharing the spoils in 2, but had only scored 319 points to Hunslet's 327, conceding 139 in comparison to 117. The Northern Union's Yorkshire Committee, however, ruled that a play-off would be necessary to determine the identity of the champions. Many observers believed that the south Leeds club should have been presented with the championship as of right, while the *Yorkshire Post* ventured: 'Serious football on the last day of April is unnatural.'

In the event, the game was played in conditions more akin to winter than summer. Bradford, who had lost 7-0 to Batley seven days earlier at the same venue in the Challenge Cup final, had beaten Wakefield Trinity on the Tuesday to force the play-off and the choice of Headingley for the game did not find universal favour.

Previewing the game, the *Yorkshire Post's* perceptive reporter reflected: 'We do not think their performance against Batley or against Wakefield Trinity augurs well for their success today. The team may do well for 20 minutes, and if they cannot get a winning lead they are not likely to get it at all, for the staleness and effect of hard work will become more apparent as the game proceeds. In the case of Hunslet, they have not had any serious football since Easter. It is a moot point whether the process of deterioration, which set in at the draw with Bradford and the defeat at Batley, has been arrested in the meantime.' He concluded: 'Hunslet will no doubt make a desperate effort to prevent the honour, which they have had seemingly safe for months, being snatched from their grasp at the last moment. We do not expect a bright and exhilarating performance from either team, but we think Hunslet should win.'

Bradford forged a 2-0 interval lead with a penalty by three-quarter Fred Cooper before a disappointing crowd of only 3,000. Hunslet captain Albert Goldthorpe could have expected some reward when, after intercepting a pass, he was obstructed by Bradford full-back Patrick in attempting to follow his subsequent kick. No penalty, however, was awarded and a huge 'rush' by the Hunslet forwards was eventually denied by opposing half-backs Calvert and Prole. Albert Goldthorpe replied in kind, saving 'in plucky fashion' when Bradford's forwards dribbled threateningly, but Hunslet were forced to concede the first minor point of the match when a beleaguered defence had to make dead a dangerous kick.

A misplaced kick by Tom Gillings gave Bradford the chance of another punt out, which Walter Goldthorpe appeared to have defused with a fair catch, only for his forwards to be caught offside and a scrummage awarded on the Hunslet line that culminated in a penalty for Bradford, which Cooper narrowly missed. Further pressure by Bradford, 'playing much the superior game', resulted

---

Hunslet 5   Bradford 2

The Hunslet side that faced Bradford's neighbours Manningham three seasons earlier, on 13 October 1894. All three teams were giants of the Northern Union, Manningham earning glory as the competition's first champions in 1895/96.

in minor points only, Hunslet's superb defence effectively winning the game in a period in which their only real respite had been a drop goal attempt by Albert Goldthorpe.

It was, however, to be a different matter in the second half. Bradford were a spent force and Hunslet, with the wind behind them, held sway, despite carrying a virtual passenger in forward T.C. 'Boxer' Young, who remained on the field despite a reported broken ankle. James Ramage, a forward capture from Gala, scored the winning try as the hour approached, Albert Goldthorpe converting.

The Parksiders returned home to memorable scenes, vividly described by the *Yorkshire Post*: 'On their return to the Anchor Hotel, Hunslet's victorious team were received with remarkable demonstrations of enthusiasm.' Flags hung from windows in the area, the footpaths were lined with jubilant supporters, and 'the Anchor Hotel was almost invisible owing to the large number of waiting friends.'

Hunslet: Mitchell, Hannah, A. Goldthorpe, W. Goldthorpe, Wright, Robinson, Gillings, Barraclough, Bowley, Deacon, Kaye, Leach, Ramage, Walsh, Young.

Bradford: Patrick, Dobson, Cooper, W. Murgatroyd, F. Murgatroyd, Calvert, Prole, Broadley, Robertson, Fearnley, Holt, Holden, Kelsey, Robinson, Foulds.

HUNSLET v. OLDHAM

Date: 29 April 1899

Location: Fallowfield, Manchester

Challenge Cup final

Referee: Mr T.H. Marshall (Bradford)

The *Yorkshire Post* had shown its faith in Hunslet's prospects and observed on the morning of the game: 'The all-important question is, Who'll win? Some Oldham people appear to have arranged that problem to their satisfaction already, judging by the fact that magisterial sanction has been asked and obtained for an extension of time this evening at a local hostelry in order that the home-brining of the cup may be fittingly celebrated. The whole incident, suggests chicken counting. There are many precedents to show that this is a risky amusement. A decade ago the famous Preston North End team had themselves photographed before the Association final tie was played, with the Cup in front of them. But neither the team nor photographer could prevent the Cup being taken by West Bromwich... we think the Cup will be won by HUNSLET.'

The *Yorkshire Post* got it wrong, failing to assess the impact of the absence of suspended half-back Tom Gillings. It was proved right, however, in its concerns over the choice of venue. The crowd of 16,000 was well down on the previous year's 'gate' of 27,000 at Headingley and the fact that Fallowfield offered generally poor viewing was held to be a factor, together with political 'infighting' between Oldham, Salford and Swinton. 'They may even try the experiment of taking the Cup Final to the Crystal Palace,' the newspaper suggested. Those who did turn up were treated to a powerful performance by Oldham, whose star player, Fletcher, predated Billy Batten in one aspect of his play. 'His habit of jumping over opponents is decidedly dangerous,' wrote the *Yorkshire Post*. 'Some say he will cripple an opponent, or suffer a broken collarbone, or worse. At the same time he is a grand player, vastly improved since he played for England, and he has given to the Oldham three-quarter line an element of dash and vigour that we do not remember to have seen in them before.

'It is also our duty to console with Hunslet in their defeat. It was their forwards who failed collectively, though individually good work was done by Ramage, Leach, O. Walsh and the others. Albert Goldthorpe was easily first in the three-quarter line. With the exception of the try scored by Walter Goldthorpe, the others failed in comparison with the Oldham three-quarters, and the joint mistake by Fletcher, W. Goldthorpe and Mitchell in the first five minutes of the match was one of those serious blunders whose influence can seldom be wiped out.'

The *Post* also reflected: 'Oldham have developed a method of their own of interpreting the punt-out rule. On several occasions, instead of making the usual lofty punt, with its resulting rush and scramble, the kicker just tipped the ball past the front line of the opposing forwards, with the view of giving his own side an opportunity of opening out a dribble. The team do not play on rule of thumb lines, but are up to all the possibilities on board.'

Hunslet had taken the lead with an early penalty by Albert Goldthorpe but a 'mutual misunderstanding' between Mitchell and Walter Goldthorpe gave Sam Lees the chance to hack on and score for Oldham, duly adding the goal. Albert Goldthorpe was narrowly wide with a shot

Hunslet 9	Oldham 19

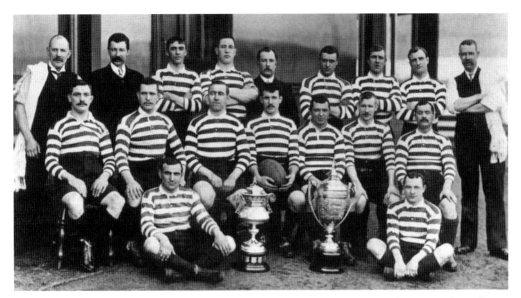

Oldham overcame Hunslet in the 1899 Challenge Cup final but the tables were turned nine years later when the consensus was that, if the Parksiders had not won all four cups that season, Oldham would have done. The Roughyeds, however, had to settle for the Lancashire Cup and the Lancashire League in 1907/08, having been denied by Hunslet in the Championship final and in the second round of the Challenge Cup. Oldham parade their two trophies.

at goal after a fair catch by James Ramage, and was unable to convert a penalty shortly after the Lancastrians' Jim Telfer was carried off after colliding with a teammate. But the centre made amends by intercepting a pass by Joe Lawton, drawing full-back R.L. Thomas before sending his brother over for a try, and also adding the extras. Albert Goldthorpe stretched the Parksiders' lead to 9-5 at half-time, successfully drop-kicking a goal when Oldham were penalised at a scrummage.

The Roughyeds, however, were to have the better of the second period once Telfer returned. Enjoying the lion's share of possession, Oldham piled on the pressure and eventually broke Hunslet's resistance, winger Sam Williams racing over in the corner after Fletcher and Sam Lee had combined. Fletcher, perhaps the best player on view, then sent Jim Moffatt over and, although Sam Lees had been unable to convert either try, the Parksiders were now behind and suffered a further mishap when Walter Goldthorpe broke his collarbone. Outnumbered, Hunslet conceded late tries from Joe Lees and Williams, Thomas adding a goal.

The decision to grant an extension at the Red Lion Hotel at Bottom 'th Moor in Oldham had been justified although there were to be repercussions, as the *Oldham Evening Chronicle* recounted in 'the story of Joe Lees' watch – stolen by a naughty, impudent, cheeky girl'; Annie Shaw, a 'well known Oldham young lady' finding herself in the dock after a night of celebrations.

Hunslet: Mitchell, Hannah, A.E. Goldthorpe, W. Goldthorpe, Wright, Robinson, Fletcher, Harrison, Leach, Ramage, Rubrey, O. Walsh, T. Walsh, Wilson, Young.

Oldham: Thomas, Davies, T. Fletcher, S. Lees, Williams, A. Lees, Lawton, Moffatt, Frater, Telfer, Bonser, Broome, Ellis, J. Lees, Barnes.

HUNSLET v. LEEDS

Date: 7 March 1903
Location: Parkside

Challenge Cup Round Three
Referee: J.H. Smith (Widnes)

The huge crowd of 22,000 that turned up at Parkside for the key Challenge Cup fixture between the two great old rivals had a major impact – according to Leeds – on the result. Over 18,000 paid for admission, with another 4,000 present either as Hunslet members or by, according to the *Yorkshire Post*, 'gaining an entrance without going through the necessary formality of paying'. Such was the pressure of the throng of spectators that pitch-side barriers cracked, 'with the result that hundreds of the spectators rushed across the field to find less embarrassing positions on the touchline side and behind the goal posts.'

Mosley, the Leeds captain, lodged an objection over the encroachment prior to the kick-off with Widnes referee Mr Smith, but play proceeded with Hunslet benefiting from a strong supporting wind. The Parksiders though were forced, against expectations, to concede a number of early scrums and Hunslet were grateful to full-back Herbert Place – the 'youthful custodian' – for a series of important tackles, catches and relieving kicks to touch.

Having withstood the onslaught, Hunslet began to exert their authority with the Goldthorpes and the Whiteleys outstanding. Albert Goldthorpe was narrowly wide with an attempted penalty when Grace was caught offside and the Loiners' response was halted when Jenkins was brought down by Whiteley. Hunslet had an escape when a rare error by Place gave Littlewood and Mosley a chance, only for the Leeds skipper to knock on with the line at his mercy. An unsuccessful long-range shot at goal by Walter Goldthorpe left the scorers still untroubled but a sustained spell of pressure by the visitors, highlighted by raids by Llewellyn, Jenkins and Mosley, was again repelled, Hunslet scrum half Everson turning the tables with a well-placed kick that outwitted Leeds' full-back Dean. Another Albert Goldthorpe drop goal attempt drifted astray of the target, Jenkins struggling to make the ball dead before the home forwards arrived, before the Parksiders took the lead in the twenty-fifth minute with the help of a finely weighted kick by 'Ahr Albert' in open play. The stand-off half, spotting possibilities on Leeds' left flank, kicked directly from a scrum on the visitors' 25-yard line. Wingers Whiteley and Jenkins were in direct competition and the tussle for the ball was won by the Hunslet man, Whiteley racing over 'in very clever fashion.' Albert Goldthorpe added the conversion from the touchline and that proved to be the end of Hunslet's scoring, but not of the drama.

Leeds attacked with a forward rush which led to Hewlett, their last man down, retiring for a spell with a knock to the head, and Albert Goldthorpe exerted renewed pressure on the Loiners' right flank, Llewellyn smothering on this occasion to ensure that the visitors trailed by only five points at the interval.

Hunslet found themselves under some pressure early in the second half when Walter Goldthorpe was caught in possession after an intelligent kick by Llewellyn. An attack by Jenkins down the left touchline was stopped by the Whiteley brothers, and J. Whiteley was again on hand when Jenkins

Hunslet 5   Leeds 2

A crowd scene from the game. The photograph – a still from the celebrated Mitchell & Kenyon collection – probably features a professional 'whipper-up', employed by the photographers.

backed up a dangerous raid by Grace. The sequel, the *Yorkshire Post* reported, was 'a hot attack on the Hunslet line, scrummage after scrummage being fought out amid the greatest excitement.' Leeds, after conceding position through an Albert Goldthorpe clearance kick, reduced the deficit when Littlewood kicked a goal after Hunslet had been penalised for obstruction; and the Loiners were grateful to right winger Evans who fell on the ball to quell a rush by the Parksiders. Albert Goldthorpe was unable to convert a penalty that could have sealed the issue, and that failure could have proved costly when Llewellyn intercepted a pass to home winger Billy Hannah, racing away and only being denied by a marvellous cover tackle as he attempted to round Place. His attack, however, set up the position for late Leeds pressure involving strong attacks on each flank, which the Hunslet defence denied for a notable win.

The Leeds Committee opted to lodge an objection, although the Loiners made no reference to the Mitchell and Kenyon photographer who is said to have entered the field of play while recording the first known moving film of a rugby game.

The *Yorkshire Post* reported: 'There is much talk in local football circles about a precedent for such an objection as that which Leeds have laid. In the Rugby Union days, it may be remembered, a similar state of things to that existing on Saturday was seen in the Cup-tie between Halifax and Hunslet. On that occasion Halifax protested, but the result was allowed to stand.' Hunslet once more had the judiciary on their side. It was held by the Northern Union's Cup Committee, which met under chairman Mr J. Clifford at the Exchange Hotel, Manchester, that although the circumstances were unusual in the history of Northern Union Cup matches, there had been no interference with play.

Hunslet: Place, J. Whiteley, H. Whiteley, W. Goldthorpe, Hannah, A.E. Goldthorpe, Everson, Shooter, Wilson, Glow, Walsh, Lunn, Tunningley, Wilcox, Brook.

Leeds: Dean, Evans, Llewellyn, Littlewood, Jenkins, Mosley, Grace, Moffat, Woolf, Taylor, Stead, Birch, Webster, Moon, Hewlett.

Halifax v. Hunslet

Date: 2 December 1905
Location: Park Avenue, Bradford

Yorkshire Cup final
Referee: Mr W. McCutchson (Oldham)

Hunslet, despite a dreadful opening, became the first winners of the Yorkshire Cup in a real clash of the titans of the Northern Union. Halifax entered the game as slight favourites, largely by virtue of the fact that they had completed the cup and league 'double' as recently as 1902/03.

The Thrum Hallers would recover the championship in 1906/07 and, with the superb Little at full-back, were generally believed to have the edge in defence. The spectators looked forward, in particular, to the clash of two mighty packs; and although the *Yorkshire Post* had little hesitation in siding with Halifax's prospects it suggested: 'It must not be forgotten that in a tight game such as this promises to be it will take very little indeed, either in the way of mistakes or luck, to turn the result either way.'

A crowd of 18,000 amassed at Park Avenue in high expectation; and the Hunslet supporters among the throng were not to be disappointed. The Parksiders, who reported the Goldthorpe brothers – Albert (who had announced his retirement towards the end of the previous season before being persuaded to return) and Walter – together with Eagers and Herbert Place fit, had reached the decider by controversial means and not without a protest from Hull KR, who had been disposed of at the penultimate stage. Hunslet, who had beaten Saville Green 14-0 at home in the first round and then hammered Keighley 37-3, also at Parkside, at the next stage, had been 12-3 ahead in Hull when fog caused the match to be abandoned in the sixty-third minute. The Yorkshire Committee ruled, to Rovers' chagrin, that the game be replayed at Parkside and Albert Goldthorpe and his men continued where they had left off, prevailing 14-3 with 2 tries for Charlie Ward, tries for William Ward and Albert Goldthorpe and a Walter Goldthorpe goal. The *Yorkshire Post* reflected: 'There will not be much doubt in the lay mind as to which of the two clubs is most entitled to figure in the final tie with Halifax. Hunslet demonstrated yesterday, even more than they did on Saturday, a superiority over Rovers which was undeniable. The superiority was reflected – and in now way exaggerated – in the result. Within a quarter of an hour from the commencement Hunslet, by dint of unusually fine concerted movement, had scored three tries and thereafter the visitors to all intents and purposes were quite "out of the hunt."'

Batley, meanwhile, were none too happy that the Yorkshire Cup final meant the postponement of their scheduled home fixture with the Parksiders, which was rearranged for Tuesday 16 January. The Gallant Youths' anguish, however, was eased when Hunslet were instructed to hand over a third of their share of the proceeds from the final.

Few neutral observers felt that the Parksiders – who, after all, had been firmly in control at Craven Park before the early stoppage – were not entitled to take their place in the decider. But there may well have been doubts when Halifax took the lead in only the second minute when, after having won a scrum on Hunslet's 25-yard line, Joe Riley, Jimmy Hilton and Wax Williams combined for W.T. Drummond to touch down, Little failing with his conversion attempt. Walter Goldthorpe

---

Halifax 3   Hunslet 13

Hunslet display their prize. From left to right, back row: Glew, Wray, Jukes, Uttley, Hannah (trainer), Williamson (trainer), Everson, Walsh, Shooter. Middle row: Eagers, Wilcox, A.E. Goldthorpe, W. Goldthorpe, Brooks, Wilson. Front row: Jackson, W. Ward, Place, C. Ward.

went close in response, being denied by Billy Wedgewood who, with his stop – which appeared to involve an element of obstruction – made up for the error that had presented the Hunslet centre with his opportunity.

Wedgewood, playing on the precipice, survived another mistake but it was third time unlucky when the Halifax three-quarter illegally halted Albert Everson, conceding the penalty that enabled Hunslet to open their account through Walter Goldthorpe, who shortly afterwards denied Wedgewood when the Thrum Hallers replied with a kick to the Parksiders' goal line.

The next score, clearly, was going to be of some importance and both Everson and Albert Goldthorpe went very close before the latter put Hunslet ahead for the first time with a typically well-taken drop goal to establish a 4-3 interval lead.

It was an advantage the Parksiders were not going to lose. Albert Goldthorpe and Little were both wide with penalty attempts but Hunslet were patently gaining the upper hand in the forwards. Another successful scrummage near the Halifax line led to 'Ahr Albert' dropping his second goal, and his brother Walter added a goal of his own after making a 'mark'. Not to be outdone, Albert bisected the uprights for the third time to extend Hunslet's lead to seven points and, with time running out, left winger Charlie Ward broke through for Hunslet's sole try of the game which, although unconverted, ensured that there was no way back for Halifax.

Halifax: Little, Hartley, Williams, Wedgewood, Drummond, Joe Riley, Hilton, Bartle, Hammond, Langhorn, Morton, Norton, Jack Riley, Swinbank, Winskill.

Hunslet: Place, C. Ward, Eagers, W. Goldthorpe, W. Ward, A.E. Goldthorpe, Everson, Shooter, Jukes, Brookes, Wray, Wilcox, Walsh, Glew.

Hunslet v. Halifax

Date: 21 December 1907

Location: Headingley, Leeds

Yorkshire Cup final

Referee: Mr W. McCutchson (Oldham)

The Parksiders enjoyed a comfortable victory in securing the first trophy of a season that would come to be regarded as one of the most remarkable in sporting history. Led by a pack of forwards that, with a fearsome reputation, earned itself the soubriquet 'The Terrible Six', Hunslet were a side that commanded respect and they had the men at the rear capable of making the most of a more-than-solid platform. Veterans Albert Goldthorpe at half-back and Walter Goldthorpe in the centre were enjoying swansongs to wonderful careers stretching back to the days before the 'Great Split' of 1895, and several of the side would be included in the inaugural Northern Union party to tour Australia in 1910. Winger Fred Farrar, stand-off Fred Smith and forward Bill Jukes would all be in that historic squad, while Hunslet had unearthed a real superstar on the wing in the immortal Billy Batten – the 'Forceful Youth from Kinsley' – who used his giant frame to power through defenders and, as a crowd-pleasing alternative, perfected the art of leaping over would-be tacklers. Batten would leave Hunslet for Hull in 1913, where he would be paid the sum of £14 per week – a huge figure in an age in which the average wage for the working man was around £1.

The securing of the Yorkshire Cup was but the first step in the Parksiders' great feat in winning every available trophy. Hunslet became the first winners of all four cups – emulated only by Huddersfield in 1914/15 and Swinton in 1927/28 – adding the Yorkshire League, the Challenge Cup and the Championship to secure true sporting glory. The Parksiders had reached the Yorkshire Cup final, and a return meeting with the Halifax side that had been accounted for at the same stage two years earlier, without having to leave their own home. Bramley had been toppled 50-0 in the first round, when Batten scored a hat-trick and Albert Goldthorpe totalled twenty-two points with two tries and eight goals, and that success was followed by another 'derby' win, Leeds going down 17-10. Wakefield Trinity, the last remaining obstacle, were denied 10-0 and the Parksiders prepared for their pre-Christmas outing with a narrow home win in the league over Huddersfield, who kept the Parksiders to a 9-7 scoreline.

Hunslet's 'Terrible Six' – essentially drawn from a pool of eight players – for the meeting with Halifax comprised Harry Wilson, Billy Brookes, Bill Jukes, Jack Randall, Tom Walsh and Walter Wray; and it was their efforts that thwarted the Thrum Hallers. Halifax, outweighed, outthought and outflanked up front, managed to win only one in six of the scrums and Albert Goldthorpe elected to make maximum use of the glut of possession by opting for a 'kick and rush' game that may not have pleased all of the 15,000 crowd but which suited the Parksiders' cause admirably. His tactics ensured that Halifax suffered a defeat described by the *Yorkshire Post* as being 'as severe as experienced for some years' and their reporter added: 'To beat a team of the calibre of Halifax by seventeen points to nil is no little achievement. One could not but admire Albert Goldthorpe's wonderful resource on the attack, again and again. His club's victory was indeed largely another personal triumph for

---

Hunslet 17   Halifax 0

'His Nibs', a popular character in the *Leeds Mercury*, offers his best wishes to Albert Goldthorpe in the bid to retain the Yorkshire Cup the following season. It wasn't to be. Halifax gained revenge in the 1908 final with a 9-5 win at Wakefield.

"Good Luck! Hunslet."

BY "THE HERMIT."

His Nibs: Ah 'ope ahsall be able ter tak another sup wi' yer in t'owd. pot at t'end o' this season, Albert.

him.' The *Leeds Mercury*, however, reflected: 'No one has greater admiration than myself for Albert Goldthorpe and I am willing to confess that, next to his forwards, he was chiefly responsible for Hunslet's victory. That being so, I suppose his kick-and-rush game will be considered justified, but my own feeling is that had he passed the ball more and kicked less, Hunslet would have won by an even greater margin, and the big crowd would have seen an exhibition of back play that would have aroused enthusiasm for the Northern Union game to a very high pitch.' 'Ahr Albert' perhaps felt that the scoreline, and the possession of the Yorkshire Cup, provided ample justification for his approach.

Hunslet had an early escape when Halifax, who lacked key three-quarters Dai Thomas (suspension) and Percy Eccles, who was ill, were unable to land a goal, Little being wide after Fred Atkins had made a 'mark'. A rush by the Parksiders' forwards was halted by Jimmy Hilton and Little thwarted a Farrar dribble, before Albert Goldthorpe put Hunslet ahead with a penalty awarded when Hilton was caught offside at a scrum. Little came close to equalising with a shot at goal from halfway, again after a 'mark', which drifted narrowly outside an upright and Hilton was only denied a try through a fine tackle by Smith. Hunslet's response, however, was swift and effective. Batten went close and Eagers, fed by Albert Goldthorpe from the scrum, dropped a goal to help his side to a 4-0 interval lead.

The scrum half extended the lead early in the second half, dribbling over direct from a scrum after Batten had again been tackled on the line, and ensured that the Parksiders remained in the ascendancy with a smart drop goal after another spell of Halifax pressure had been repelled. The Captain Fantastic went on to supply the final pass for Smith to race over, and then sparked a move involving Smith and Charlie Ward that secured a richly deserved try for Batten. Neither score was converted but, in the meantime, Charlie Ward had kept the momentum going with a drop goal to seal Hunslet's win.

Hunslet: Place, Farrar, C. Ward, Eagers, Batten, A.E. Goldthorpe, Smith, Wilson, Brookes, Jukes, Randall, Walsh, W. Wray.

Halifax: Little, Morley, Atkins, Ward, Riley, Hilton, Grey, Brearley, Hammond, Robinson, Littlewood, Langhorn, Sunderland.

HUNSLET v. NEW ZEALAND

Date: 26 December 1907
Location: Parkside

Tour match
Referee: Mr W. McCutcheon (Oldham)

Hunslet, during the season in which they won all four cups, had the honour of meeting and entertaining the first touring side to these shores, A.H. Baskerville's famous New Zealand 'All Golds', on their arrival in the north of England. The Parksiders' standing in the game was such that the Hunslet club was asked to fete the pioneers who, after having been met initially by five members of the Northern Union committee on docking at Folkestone on 30 September 1907, travelled to Leeds the following day.

The *Yorkshire Post* reported: 'There was a tremendous crowd in City Square. The Hunslet Club had driven to the station in a decorated char-a-banc, which bore the emblem "Hunslet welcome the New Zealand team." When the players appeared the crowd burst into tremendous cheering, which continued until the men got into their char-a-banc. Then Wright, the New Zealand captain, called for "Three cheers for the people of Leeds," which were followed by the stirring Maori war cry and further cheering. The players were escorted to the Grand Central Hotel by the Hunslet char-a-banc and the Northern Union officials in carriages, together with the still cheering crowd. The crush was so dense in Boar Lane and Briggate as to cause a stoppage of all traffic. Outside the hotel the team were again prevailed upon to give a rendition of the Maori war cry, while as they made their way into the hotel they were greeted by further cheering and the strains of *"God Save the King."* It was a stirring scene.'

It was a stirring scene nearly three months later when the All Golds arrived at Parkside for their Boxing Day match with Hunslet; a game classed in some circles as an extra 'Test', although New Zealand had slipped a little after a ten-match unbeaten opening to the tour. That fine start had dissolved into a mixed record. Of the thirteen subsequent games prior to the date at Hunslet, the All Golds had won just five – and it was seen as imperative for the health of the tour that a good result was secured against a team that could justifiably describe itself as the pride of the Northern Union. The fixture pitted together several of the 'greats', with the Australian three-quarter Dally Messenger playing for New Zealand, the immortal Lance Todd starring on the wing, and Albert Goldthorpe displaying his skills at stand-off half for the Parksiders.

Hunslet went into the Thursday afternoon game on the back of a busy schedule. The side had beaten Halifax the previous Saturday to win the Yorkshire Cup, and had met the Thrum Hallers again, at Parkside, on Christmas Day. New Zealand presented stiff opposition twenty-four hours later and what would have been a daunting schedule for any team closed with the visit of Wigan on the Saturday.

Hunslet weren't fazed – and nor were their supporters. A crowd of 15,000 turned up for the Yorkshire Cup final at Headingley, 9,000 paid to see the Christmas Day fixture and an attendance of 19,000 was recorded at Parkside for a glimpse of Baskerville's pioneers. They were not to be

Hunslet 11

New Zealand 11

Albert Goldthorpe, the master of the drop goal, secured a notable draw against the All Golds with a typical effort. A cartoonist captures his affectation of dipping his hand as the ball traversed the crossbar.

New Zealand stand-off Edgar Wrigley, who exchanged shirts with Albert Goldthorpe at the end of the game, was impressed by Hunslet, joining the Parksiders in 1913 after spell with Huddersfield. Wrigley is pictured fourth from left in the second row from the back.

disappointed – although the Hunslet committee may have pondered on the wisdom of agreeing a pooled 'gate' with their neighbours at Headingley, who had only attracted 12,321 for their earlier fixture with the tourists – and it was to be a similar story on the Saturday when 8,000 eased through the turnstiles for the 12-11 win over Wigan. Those supporters, in what was described as a strongly partisan crowd, who were determined on a Hunslet victory may have been a shade concerned at the interval, when New Zealand had established a nine-point lead with a try and a goal by stand-off Edgar Wrigley (the 'Village Blacksmith') and two goals for Messenger. The only joy for the Parksiders in the opening period had been the pre-match performance of the 'Haka' – the Maori war dance – but, with Albert Goldthorpe to the fore, Hunslet had much the better of the second half.

31

HUNSLET v. NEW ZEALAND

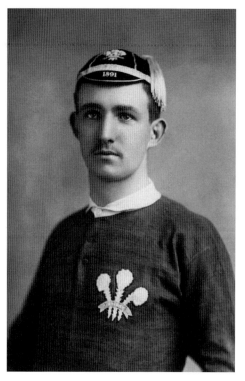

Left: Referee Bill McCutcheon, the great Welsh centre who had joined Oldham in 1888 before picking up the whistle on his retirement in 1897, was at the centre of controversy when he ruled that the immortal Dally Messenger had not played the ball correctly. Albert Goldthorpe kicked what proved to be an important penalty in the 11-11 draw.

Opposite: Hunslet proudly pose with the 1907/08 Yorkshire Cup, won less than a week before the fixture with New Zealand. More silver was on its way. From left to right, back row: W.H. Cockeram (Secretary), Smales, Farrar, Higson, W. Hannah (Trainer), Wilson, Wray, Cappleman, J. Lewthwaite (Chairman). Middle row: Eagers, Randall, W. Ward, A.E. Goldthorpe (captain), Jukes, Brookes, W. Goldthorpe. Front row: C. Ward, Place, Smith, Walsh.

Goldthorpe, indeed, was crucial to the victory (despite having elected to play against the wind in the first half). Yet he came very close to not playing. Flaneur of the *Leeds Mercury* reported: 'It would have been a calamity for Hunslet had Albert Goldthorpe not turned out, and probably few of that great crowd know how near their idol was to watching the game from the committee stand. As a fact, Goldthorpe was suffering from an injury to his leg, and was limping about the pavilion declaring that he was not really fit to turn out. But so great is the faith of his men in their leader that the Hunslet players with one accord endeavoured to induce him to play, and they were successful.'

That was hardly surprising. Goldthorpe, a central figure in the Yorkshire Cup win, had again been Halifax's main tormentor when the sides renewed acquaintance four days later in the Christmas Day league fixture. The teams appeared to be heading for what most observers felt would have been a merited draw when the living legend kicked a wonderful drop goal from a position measured as fifteen yards from the corner flag to snatch an 8-6 win. The *Halifax Daily Guardian* reflected: 'It was only after they had been out of the hunt for the last quarter that they managed to get up an attack for Albert Goldthorpe to drop a remarkable goal, the more surprising since he was literally surrounded by opponents. But then that is Albert all over.' And the *Yorkshire Post*, suggesting that a draw would have been a fair result, reported that 'a wonderful drop goal by Albert Goldthorpe had won it. There was an element of good fortune about the goal, but it was an effort that was characteristic of the versatile Hunslet veteran.'

Hunslet's only absentee was winger Fred Farrar, while New Zealand badly missed impressive three-quarter George Smith, whose unavailability with a rib injury left Messenger and W.T. 'Cork'

Wynyard starved of possession on the wings. The Parksiders, felt by Flaneur to have been fortunate not to have lost the game, overcame the dismissal of Smith for kicking grounded New Zealand captain Hercules R. 'Bumper' Wright to claw their way back into the contest with four goals by Goldthorpe. One penalty, awarded against Messenger for not playing the ball correctly, was felt to be contentious, Flaneur reporting: 'This decision hinged on a very small point. Messenger was tackled in possession, and was thrown on his back. The ball was not held, nor did it appear to touch the ground, and Messenger passed it back to a colleague. For this he was penalised, Mr McCutcheon apparently holding that the ball had touched the ground, in which case Messenger should have got up and played it with his foot.'

Dally Messenger, however, seemed to have won the game for the All Golds with a penalty from the halfway line but the decision to disallow an earlier 'try' – Mr McCutcheon ruling a forward pass by Wynyard before Messenger crossed – proved costly. And Hunslet squared the issue with a pushover try for Wilson, which Flaneur again questioned for offside. Goldthorpe's conversion attempt, however, drifted a couple of inches wide, leaving honours even and the spectators treated to yet another stirring scene as Wrigley asked Goldthorpe for his jersey. 'As generous as ever,' wrote Flaneur, 'Albert disrobed on the field and ran through the crowd to the dressing room uncovered to the waist, while Wrigley waved the white jersey aloft in triumph.' Wrigley subsequently wore the white jersey on his own account, joining Hunslet from Huddersfield in 1913/14.

Hunslet: Place, C. Ward, W. Goldthorpe, Eagers, Batten, A.E. Goldthorpe, Smith, Wilson, Brookes, Randall, Walsh, W. Wray, Jukes.

New Zealand: Turtill, Messenger, Rowe, W. Wynyard, Todd, Wrigley, R. Wynyard, Gilchrist, Pearce, Cross, Byrne, Wright, Johnstone.

LEEDS v. HUNSLET

Date: 29 February 1908
Location: Headingley, Leeds

Challenge Cup first round
Referee: Mr E. Tonge (Swinton)

Hunslet safely circumvented the hurdle of their neighbours with yet another derby victory that clearly concerned the *Leeds Mercury*'s Flaneur. Leeds were to finish the season in twentieth position, compared to Hunslet's second spot, and the Loiners' continuing role as rubbing rags to their eminent neighbours was beginning to vex the scribe. He wrote: 'The eagerly anticipated Northern Union Cup match between Leeds and Hunslet ended in the usual way, the Parksiders, after experiencing rather an anxious hour, finally arising in their might and smiting their local rivals.

'I do not mind admitting that the result was a personal disappointment to me, as it probably was to the majority of the fine crowd of twelve thousand people, who showed by their presence on a wretched afternoon that there is still a public for Northern Union football in Leeds.'

Flaneur continued: 'Lest I should be accused of partisanship, I would hasten to add that my desire for a Leeds success was not based on club preference – I have no favourite team in any code of football – it was based on the broad lines of the greatest good for the Northern Union game in the city.

'Though the Hunslet crowd are notoriously fickle, a defeat for the Parksiders could have been borne with equanimity, seeing that Hunslet are already the holders of the Yorkshire Senior Cup and are in the running for the league championship. But with Leeds the case is different. The club have never won a Cup tournament; they have never beaten Hunslet in a Cup-tie; and they have now nothing to play for this season. A victory on Saturday would have done the Leeds club and Northern Unionism in the city a world of good, and it was for that reason I had hoped Leeds would, at long last, create a precedent in their Cup matches with their neighbours.'

Flaneur added: 'Then, too, the sportsman has a natural leaning to the "under dog", and it was this sympathy that caused one, against one's better judgment, to anticipate a Leeds victory. For more than an hour the Leeds men did much to encourage their supporters, though their backs lacked the finish and "class" generally that makes the difference between a mediocre and a good side. One felt that a lead of five points at the interval, after a spell of forty minutes with a strong wind at their backs, was not sufficient to give Leeds the victory, and immediately Hunslet drew level the game was all over bar the shouting.

'The collapse of the home team from the moment they were overtaken was nothing short of tragic. They had played, or their forwards, at least, had played for three-quarters of the game with a grim earnestness that merited a more substantial score than five points, and the reaction came with a vengeance when Albert Goldthorpe steered the ball between the posts from a somewhat lucky try by Jukes, and made the scores five points all.'

That try, lucky or not – and Flaneur conceded that Leeds' own score, by centre Thomas with full-back Young adding the conversion, owed something to good fortune – resulted from the Parksiders' first real attack after having been under the cosh throughout the first half. Billy Batten, switched from

---

Leeds 5   Hunslet 14

LEEDS v. HUNSLET

An artist reviews the action.

[Within illustration:] HUNSLET DEFEAT LEEDS — Batten daringly stopped an ominous rush — Leeds try — Young opened the scoring — Jukes went three quarter's & turned the tide with a clever entry — Batley & Wadd receive Notice to Quit — The joy of Randall on Jukes' scoring a try — Wilson passed to Tubby Brookes who hurled himself over the line! — Eason 1900

the wing to full-back because of Place's suspension, was an heroic figure, three times going down amid flying feet to prevent tries, while Loiners winger Ward was judged to have stepped into touch before crossing in the corner. Hunslet also possibly benefited from the dismissals of Batten and Leeds' Wade for fighting. The Parksiders switched Eagers to full-back who 'proved as great a full-back as Batten, and Jukes fitted well into the three-quarter line. On the other hand, Webster, a magnificent forward, has not even a smattering of three-quarter play, and the Leeds back play, never good, was painfully ineffective in the second half, while Webster was badly missed from the forwards.'

Hunslet went on to dominate the closing quarter, ending Leeds' hopes with three quick tries. One, for winger William Ward owed much, Flaneur conceded, to the 'superb judgment of Albert Goldthorpe and the skill of the two Wards in handling the greasy ball'. That score was preceded by touchdowns for heavyweight forward Bill 'Tubby' Brookes, who powered over from a fine pass by Harry Wilson, and a try for Wilson himself.

Wrote Flaneur: 'One must heartily congratulate the winners. They seemed severely handicapped in the absence of Place and Walter Goldthorpe, who is suffering from influenza, but the two Wards, who came into the three-quarter line to fill the gaps, played very well indeed and Walter Goldthorpe and Batten could not have improved on the finest try of the match.

'Under Albert Goldthorpe's generalship the Hunslet men played a masterly game. One can imagine Albert remarking in his quiet way, when Hunslet had drawn level, "Now's our chance, lads." And how magnificently the team responded! There were no half measures. It was like a winning boxer weakening his opponent by knocking him down each time he staggers up to the count. There was no quarter, and in the final stages Leeds had thrown up the sponge.'

Leeds: Young, Ward, Thomas, Wade, Desborough, Wilson, Burgess, Birch, Webster, Harrison, Ibbitson, Brown, Lunn.

Hunslet: Batten, W. Ward, C. Ward, Eagers, Farrar, A.E. Goldthorpe, Smith, Wilson, Brookes, Randall, Higson, Smales, Jukes.

35

HUNSLET v. OLDHAM

Date: 14 March 1908

Location: Parkside

Challenge Cup second round

Referee: Mr F. Kennedy (Broughton)

Oldham, generally regarded as Hunslet's main challengers in the bid to become the first team to win all four cups, had their hopes dashed in the early stages of the code's glamour competition. Perhaps significantly, the Parksiders secured a place in the third round despite being without captain Albert Goldthorpe. The mercurial half-back, who had been struggling with a thigh injury since Christmas when he had turned out against New Zealand with the greatest reluctance, finally had to bow to nature after intensive treatment by a specialist failed to cure the problem prior to the biggest tie of the round. A crowd of 20,000, paying £610, turned up for the game with many fearing the worst in the absence of 'Ahr Albert'.

Goldthorpe's deputy, Fred Whittaker, had to cry off with influenza and the Parksiders opted to switch Bill Jukes from the forwards to share the half-back duties with Fred Smith. It was the second successive cup-tie in which Jukes found himself playing out of position. The talented scrummager had been withdrawn into the centres a fortnight earlier at Headingley, following Billy Batten's dismissal against Leeds, and his input had been hugely influential in Hunslet's eventually comfortable win. The ploy also worked against Oldham, who were at full strength apart from long-term absentee Arthur Oldershaw. The visitors, who had already lifted the Lancashire Cup with a 16-9 win over Broughton Rangers at Rochdale, would also secure the Lancashire League and the subsequent defeat by Hunslet in the Championship final would add credence to the view that if the Parksiders hadn't won all four cups, Oldham – who finished the season as league leaders – would have done. Despite the efforts of Jukes, Oldham's glittering back play on a fine day suggested that it could be the Lancastrians, rather than Hunslet, who would prevail and the belief was that the side with the superior staying power would reach the quarter-finals.

That proved to be the Parksiders who, having repelled an early storm, began to assert their authority up front, where their forwards tested the Oldham defence with a series of rushes. Centre Billy Eagers opened Hunslet's account with a score that may, later, have brought a rebuke or at the very least an acidic observation from his watching captain. According to the *Yorkshire Post*: 'Eagers smartly picked up the ball, and appeared to be going straight for the line. He had two men on his right, but when going at full speed, he took a drop at goal, and the ball sailed between the posts. The two points gave unbounded satisfaction to the Hunslet supporters, but it was clearly a case of bad football producing an unexpected success.'

Eagers may have quickly regretted his decision to ignore what had been a clear try-scoring opportunity that could have put his side five points ahead instead of a mere two. Oldham hit back immediately, Scottish forward Bert Avery charging down Herbert Place's attempted clearing kick for a try. Joe Ferguson, unable to improve, added a penalty shortly afterwards, but Hunslet centre Walter Goldthorpe quickly reduced the deficit to a single point. The visitors, however, confirmed their

---

Hunslet 15   Oldham 8

Hunslet issued commemorative inset photographs of each of the 1907/08 squad with all four cups. Bill Jukes, a formidable member of the Terrible Six, could also play in the backs and excelled at stand-off against Oldham.

fine pedigree with the try of the game to take an 8-4 lead at the interval. Stand-off White broke clear, reaching Place before feeding right centre Dixon, who handed on to Llewellyn, the former Leeds centre scorching over for an unconverted touchdown.

Hunslet, however, were to take command in the second period, Flaneur of the *Leeds Mercury* reflecting: 'The staying power of the Hunslet forwards is little short of marvellous. For eighty minutes they were going at top pressure, yet their last rush was as vigorous and as dangerous as their first.' The Parksiders were firmly back in the frame within two minutes of the resumption. Eagers made an early break and on this occasion opted to pass rather than kick for goal. Wilson, on hand as usual, kept the move going by feeding Jukes who, using Batten as a foil, outfoxed Oldham winger Tyson by returning the ball to Wilson, who galloped over unopposed. Goldthorpe was again unable to add the extras but Hunslet were now on the rampage and retrieved the lead ten minutes into the half when Jukes scuttled around a scrum, finding Eagers who sent winger Farrar in at the corner for another unconverted score. Farrar, who had taken his try very cleverly, wrapped up Hunslet's success with a solo touchdown of the highest order. The winger, collecting a clearance kick by Thomas at high speed, rounded opposite number Yewlett and Llewellyn with the greatest of ease, grounding behind the posts to a rousing reception to give Goldthorpe an easy conversion.

The Parksiders also had much to celebrate off the field. The match had attracted the biggest crowd of the day, the attendance beating the 17,000 at Broughton v. Wigan by 3,000. Hull pulled in 12,000 for their tussle with Salford; that figure was also returned at Mount Pleasant for Batley's clash with Wakefield Trinity, and there was a 10,000 gate at the derby between Runcorn and Warrington.

The *Yorkshire Evening Post* enthused: 'Hunslet are undoubtedly to be looked upon as the finest all-round team in Yorkshire.'

Hunslet: Place, Batten, W. Goldthorpe, Eagers, Farrar, Jukes, Smith, Wilson, Brookes, Randall, Walsh, Smales, Higson.

Oldham: Thomas, Tyson, Dixon, Llewellyn, Yewlett, White, Benyon, Ferguson, Smith, Avery, Topham, Wilkinson, Longworth.

Barrow v. Hunslet

Date: 28 March 1908

Location: Cavendish Park, Barrow

Challenge Cup third round

The *Yorkshire Post*, in looking ahead to the Parksiders' quarter-final tie in north-west Lancashire, had asserted that Hunslet had a 'very stiff task' before them, with the rider that, on league form, the south Leeds club were 'much the better side'. Hunslet prepared thoroughly by staying at Furness Abbey the night before the game, while around 700 supporters followed on the day of the match on a special train chartered with the Midland Railway Company. Those fans were heavily outnumbered in the 12,000 crowd but played their part in a victory that some in Barrow reckoned could have been pre-ordained.

The Shipbuilders were unsettled by the fact that the town hall flag was flying at half mast out of respect for the late Duke of Devonshire, who had given Barrow their ground and in whose family name the stadium had been commemorated. Legend had it that the Barrow team only played well when within sight of the town hall clock and there were those locally who feared that, if it were to be obscured by the flag, Hunslet would progress to the semi-finals. In the event there was, Albion of the *Leeds Mercury* recorded, an 'uninterrupted view of the dial' and, regardless of superstition, the quality of the Parksiders' squad was the determining factor as Albion, 'a member of the gay party from Leeds', confirmed; despite the fact that Barrow – who had achieved something that had been beyond Hunslet in overcoming the New Zealand tourists – boasted an active pack and backs of renown in John Wharton, Harry Gifford and Ted Brockbank.

Hunslet had left a spot of trouble behind in Leeds where the club had instigated criminal proceedings against a spectator, one John Thomas Arundale, who had kicked the referee on the shin following the previous Monday evening's 5-3 win over Merthyr Tydfil at Parkside, when John Willie Higson had been sent off by the referee, Mr William Henry Wood of Lindley. A small section of the crowd had, according to the *Leeds Mercury*, 'favoured the referee with a systematic course of booing' and had 'got onto the field and gathered round him, displaying hostility. The defendant deliberately kicked the referee on the shin. The kick was not a very severe one, but its severity lay in the fact that referees must be protected when discharging their duties to the best of their ability. Wood seized the defendant, who was got into the pavilion where he said he was exceedingly sorry for what he had done. He suggested that he had been forced forward by the crowd and in the rush his foot accidentally came in contact with the complainant's leg.'

The summons was withdrawn on the basis that Arundale had been suitably apologetic, but not before the court heard that Mr Wood had been involved in an incident as a touch judge when Bradford Northern had played at Parkside in January. Asked if, on that occasion, he had 'deliberately turned to a stand full of people, and put your fingers to your nose?' he replied, 'No, I was blowing my nose.' When asked, 'You don't expect a continuous round of applause?' Mr Wood responded, 'No, I take it as a compliment, this booing.'

Barrow 0

Hunslet 8

Barrow v. Hunslet

Bill 'Tubby' Brookes, a massive presence in the formidable Hunslet pack.

There was little reason for Hunslet supporters to boo the match official at Barrow. The home side, after a promising opening quarter, rarely threatened against a Parkside team facing a strong sun and slight crosswind. Hunslet established a three-point interval lead through a try by Billy Batten, who made sure that intelligent approach play by half back Smith and Walter Goldthorpe wasn't wasted, while Albion reflected that Barrow may have prospered more from a more positive approach. 'After all,' he wrote, 'the best defence lies in attack, and had they not overvalued the strength of the other side, and pinned their faith in themselves, it is not at all certain that the balance at the interval would have lain with the Yorkshiremen.'

Barrow, once adrift, were fighting a lost cause. Albert Goldthorpe, who otherwise had a relatively quiet game, stretched Hunslet's lead with a drop goal, and a semi-final berth was duly booked when Smales scored a try after an error by home stand-off Wharton.

The following Wednesday Hunslet returned to league action, winning 4-3 at home to Batley and prevailing 8-5 at Dewsbury on the Saturday to seal second place in the table and ratify the Yorkshire League championship. Flaneur, of the *Leeds Mercury*, wrote: 'They can now afford to lose at Wigan following their cup tie on the same ground.

'What a remarkable difference between the performances of Hunslet and Leeds this season! Surely Leeds, in allowing Halifax to score 10 tries against them on Saturday, have touched the lowest depths of misery. Their committee and members will be glad when the closure is put on this season's dreadful performance, and a fresh start can be made in September. In the meantime some scouting and some money will be necessary.'

Barrow: Logan, Fox, Gifford, McKenny, E. Brockbank, Wharton, Barnes, Bowers, Huggett, Hall, Hannah, J. Brockbank, Brough.

Hunslet: Place, Farrar, Eagers, W. Goldthorpe, Batten, Smith, A.E. Goldthorpe, Wilson, Brookes, Jukes, Randall, Smales, Walsh.

Broughton Rangers v. Hunslet

Date: 11 April 1908

Location: Central Park, Wigan

Challenge Cup semi-final

Referee: Mr R. Robinson (Bradford)

Broughton Rangers, who had been the first side to record the cup and league 'double' six years earlier, represented for that reason the best opposition to be disposed of at the penultimate stage of each competition as Hunslet continued their assault on all four cups. Rangers, with the great Bob Wilson as skipper, were in confident mood in the build up to the game but the Manchester outfit's hopes were ultimately thwarted by a fine display from the Terrible Six after meticulous preparations by trainer Billy Hannah, the winger who had joined Hunslet the season before the split from Cumberland and never returned home. The Parksiders travelled early to Wigan, booking into their hotel where the players spent a couple of hours resting in bed. The approach paid dividends as Rangers' speedy backs were kept in check throughout by a Hunslet pack which perhaps gave its greatest performance of many.

'What must be said of the forwards?' rejoiced the *Leeds Mercury*. 'Fine pack as they are, Harry Wilson and co. perhaps excelled themselves. In the art of securing possession they were masters, while they were certainly not worsted in the loose. It would be unfair to say that the main credit for the victory should be laid at their door, but they certainly are entitled to all praise for their splendid efforts.'

Hunslet's backs also showed themselves to be at the very least the equals of their redoubtable opponents, with full-back Herbert Place particularly outstanding, and perhaps the highest accolade came from the *Leeds Mercury* which reflected of Broughton: 'It can be said of them that they lasted to the end. In this it must be understood that, while playing a poor second to their opponents, there was no slackening off, even when in the last twenty minutes of the game Hunslet were piling on the points. No quarter was given or asked by either team, and it says much for the sportsmanlike qualities of the players that the referee had only once to admonish a warning for an excess of zeal.'

The game started badly for Hunslet, who fell behind to a penalty goal by Rangers' full-back Billy Barlow, but centre Billy Eagers responded by using his winger Fred Farrar as a decoy, bisecting Wilson and Andrew Hogg to send Farrar away. The winger rounded his opposite number, Claude James, and then left Barlow trailing for a superb try that, although unconverted, gave the Parksiders a one-point advantage at the break. Hunslet, with that boost, were generally on top in a second half in which one or two veterans in the Broughton side, notably Wilson and Hogg, served evidence of their declining years. The *Leeds Mercury* reported: 'Wilson is not the brilliant centre of a few seasons ago. In common with Hogg, and particularly Flynn, he played into Hunslet's hands by incessant kicking when passing would have served a much better purpose.

'The Hunslet players were triers to a man and if one singles out Place and Albert Goldthorpe it is because the former proved invaluable on the defence, and the veteran initiated many of the moves that led to the scores. The coolness of the supreme master's hand was ever noticeable.'

Broughton Rangers 2   Hunslet 16

BROUGHTON RANGERS v. HUNSLET

Hunslet were lauded after the convincing Challenge Cup semi-final victory over Broughton. The Parksiders were to make an even bigger impression seven days later in the championship play-offs!

Powerful winger Billy Batten regularly had the 16,000 crowd on its feet with his blockbusting runs down the touchline, and Broughton were unable to prevent him from forcing his way over for a well-deserved try. Half-back Smith, meanwhile, caused the Manchester men incessant problems around the scrum and grabbed two important touchdowns. Albert Goldthorpe added a goal and a drop goal, passing the 800-goal mark for the club in the process, to put the game beyond Broughton and secure Hunslet a place in the Challenge Cup final for the first time in nine years.

'It must have been a revelation to Bob Wilson to see his fellow backs hopelessly at a loss to make any headway against the robust attention paid them by the Parkside forwards,' stated Forward of the *Leeds Mercury*, and Wilson and his colleagues must of necessity have been worried in contemplating the visit to Hunslet, seven days later, in the Championship semi final. A saving grace for Broughton, perhaps, was that the Parksiders, by a quirk of the fixture list, had to return to Wigan only two days later for an outstanding league fixture. The committee, understandably, selected a weakened side for the trip and, after losing 36-0, was duly reported and fined £10. The *Leeds Mercury*, however, stood Hunslet's corner, its reporter arguing: 'I should fancy the side that met Wigan against the majority of Yorkshire Northern League clubs. A back division including Batten, Eagers, the two Wards, Hoyle, Smith and Whittaker is not weak, and, with the exception of the last-named, every one of these players has taken part in one or other of the big matches against Leeds this season. Again, with about one exception, all the forwards that played were men of considerable first-team experience.

'As a fact, Hunslet can put two strong teams into the field, and the men who played against Wigan seemed capable of putting up a better fight. I do not think the Cup team, after their big effort of the previous Saturday, would have given any more successful exhibition.'

Broughton Rangers: Barlow, C. James, Hogg, Wilson, Hardyman, S. James, Flynn, Clampitt, Mottram, Darlinson, Beetham, Winskill, Ruddick.

Hunslet: Place, Farrar, Eagers, W. Goldthorpe, Batten, A.E. Goldthorpe, Smith, Wilson, Brookes, Jukes, Randall, Smales, Walsh.

Hunslet v. Broughton Rangers

Date: 18 April 1908   Championship semi-final
Location: Parkside   **Referee:** Mr J.H. Smith (Widnes)

Any worries of a backlash against Broughton following the Challenge Cup semi-final victory seven days earlier came to nothing as the Parksiders hit the heights with a sensational display. Rangers lacked several of the previous week's side, with wingers Claude James and Hardyman out of the side and stand-off Sam James another absentee – forcing forwards George Mottram and Billy Winskill out into the backs. Those changes, however, only went part way to explaining why Hunslet's victory was so emphatic, particularly as the Parksiders had been held to a 5-0 lead at half-time.

Albert Goldthorpe and his men simply cut loose in the second period, with the captain's oft-favoured tactic of deploying his forwards in a kick-and-rush game (the ploy of dribbling forward with the ball at their feet) reaping rich reward. The *Manchester Guardian*, pontificating on the crucial period before the hour, lamented: 'Much of the success of Hunslet was due to the splendid work of the forwards who had a much larger say in the rout than they had at Wigan, the robust rushes and brilliant dribbling completely nonplussing the Broughton Lion.'

The *Leeds Mercury* reflected: 'Broughton were not merely defeated, they were put to the rout, and one had to rub one's eyes to realise that the Rangers team included a few of the players who represented the club that won the League Championship and the Northern Union Cup in 1901/02. It is questionable if any Northern Union club has been responsible for more consistently brilliant football than the Broughton team of that season.

'What a fall from greatness! What a humiliation to be smitten hip and thigh by a side that did not play their strongest game – for Hunslet developed a lot of slackness when they had made the issue quite safe – to be toyed with and made to look little better than schoolboys. It was surely one of the darkest days the Broughton Rangers' managers have ever known!'

Of the Parksiders, the *Mercury's* scribe enthused: 'Hunslet are undoubtedly the team of the season. I question whether the club have ever had a better side.

'In the early 'nineties, when Albert and Walter Goldthorpe were younger than they are now, when James Goldthorpe and Matt Carr, Lapping and Townend, were other stars of the back division, and when Hunslet won the Yorkshire Challenge Cup, the Parksiders were a great force in the football of the North. Later, in the days of Mitchell, Hannah, Jack Wright, Robinson, Gillings, and again, of course, Albert and Walter Goldthorpe, the Parksiders were great performers, but the present side can, I think, more than challenge comparison with the fine teams of the past. At all events, Hunslet are winding up the greatest season in their history.'

He added: 'It may be thought that I am changing my ground after fancying Broughton against Hunslet at Wigan in the Cup semi-final. My chief reason for doubting Hunslet on that occasion was the fact that the match was at Wigan, where the Parksiders had rarely done themselves anything like justice. I also thought that, after their great efforts through the season, they might show signs of staleness.'

Hunslet 28   Broughton Rangers 3

HUNSLET v. BROUGHTON RANGERS

Tom Walsh, a proud member
of the Terrible Six.

'Since seeing them beat the Broughton men at Parkside in the League semi-final, I have no fear of staleness. If pushed they are capable of going at top pressure up to the last minute, and I fancy they will put on something like a record score for a Cup Final at Huddersfield next week, and wind up the season by beating Oldham in the final for the League championship.

'It would seem that Hunslet's period of adversity in the early part of the year, when they lost several league matches in succession, has really been a good thing for the team. They have certainly come up to the scratch like giants refreshed and the stiffer the hurdle that confronts them the better they seem to play. It will be a keen disappointment in Leeds if the Parksiders do not emulate the performance of Broughton Rangers in 1901/02, and of Halifax in 1902/03, and win the double events.'

Hunslet were on the brink of greatness after Broughton, who were without stand-off Jack Flynn for half an hour in the first half because of injury and who had played into the wind in the opening period, fell away after having limited the Parksiders to a Jack Randall try and Albert Goldthorpe conversion. Goldthorpe's men went on to add a point a minute by the hour, with Rangers' defenders failing to go down to halt Hunslet's numerous rushes and only Andrew Hogg and Billy Barlow showing any taste for the fight. Bob Wilson 'took flying kicks at nothing', Harris was 'no more than moderate' and Flynn 'did nothing but kick'. Winskill and Mottram, meanwhile, were out of their depth out of the pack. Wrote Flaneur: 'They use their brains, these Hunslet backs, and I do not know a player in Yorkshire I would substitute for any one of the seven who played on Saturday.'

Broughton, against that background, had to be content with a late consolation try by Jim Clampitt, who was sent over by the resilient Hogg after Hunslet, with the match won and two finals on the horizon, eased off. The Parksiders, meanwhile, had reached their first championship final with the help of tries by Fred Farrar, John Willie Higson, Fred Smith, Billy Brookes and Bill Jukes, with Goldthorpe completing a five-goal haul.

Hunslet: Place, Farrar, Eagers, W. Goldthorpe, Batten, Smith, A.E. Goldthorpe, Wilson, Jukes, Randall, Higson, Brookes, Walsh.

Broughton Rangers: Barlow, Harris, Hogg, Wilson, Mottram, Flynn, Winskill, Ruddick, Scott, Oram, Beetham, Clampitt, Grainey.

Hull v. Hunslet

Date: 25 April 1908

Location: Fartown, Huddersfield

Challenge Cup final

Referee: Mr J.H. Smith (Widnes)

The thoughts of older supporters inevitably turned to the 1892 Yorkshire Cup final when the venue was announced for the meeting with Hull. Fartown, which had provided the stage for the meeting with Leeds sixteen years earlier, had unaccountably been overlooked for any final since that memorable occasion, when Hunslet had won their first major trophy, and two men in particular were entitled to look back with more fondness than most as they anticipated a return.

The *Yorkshire Evening Post*, in backing Hunslet, wrote: 'If anyone who saw Hunslet win that Cup Final at Huddersfield 16 years ago had ventured the prophesy that two members of the victorious team, Albert and Walter Goldthorpe, would wear the same club jerseys in another final in 1908 he would have been looked upon as a very eligible candidate for Colney Hatch – or its Wharfedale equivalent.'

The *Leeds Mercury*, looking forward to the first all-Yorkshire Challenge Cup final since Batley and Bradford had met at Headingley ten years earlier, also supported Hunslet's bid. Their writer Flaneur stated: 'Hull have a great full-back and two clever half backs, but their forwards, on the showing in the semi-final at Halifax, are only moderate, and their three-quarter line is no better.

'Hunslet have a finely balanced team in all departments. Hull have been in special training during the week; the Hunslet men have, as usual, been following their daily toil. The odds are on the toilers.'

The Parksiders justified the stance of the pundits with a comfortable victory in a game played in unseasonable snowstorms, which reduced the attendance to 18,000. The pitch, too, was described as 'very heavy and holding, a ground that militated entirely against good football' and on this occasion it was Hunslet's backs, rather than the renowned 'Terrible Six' up front, who primarily set the defensive lead. Fred Smith and Billy Batten tackled ferociously throughout, while Herbert Place was in fine form at full-back, matching the 'great Hull custodian' Harry Taylor, who was playing in his first final after a glorious twelve-year career previously bereft of any medals whatsoever. 'There was nothing showy about his work,' wrote Flaneur, 'but he did everything he was called upon to do with coolness, ease, and neatness. In a trying cup-tie Place has probably no superior among Northern Union full-backs.'

Cumbrian centre Bill Eagers, the only non-Yorkshireman in the side, put Hunslet ahead with a drop goal and that score was followed by a bustling try for Smith – 'the type,' wrote the *Leeds Mercury's* Flaneur, 'only possible to a half back of the sturdy, determined and dashing sort'. Albert Goldthorpe added the conversion to secure a seven-point interval lead and landed another goal in the second half from a mark made by Smith. Winger Fred Farrar latched onto Eagers' intelligent cross-kick to record Hunslet's second try and Goldthorpe improved with his ninety-sixth goal of the season. Flaneur, speculating that Albert Goldthorpe could retire at the end of his twentieth campaign, wrote: 'Albert is by no means done yet, and one could not help admiring his artistry again on Saturday. Some of his work did not make for a very attractive game, but in everything he did one could see that there was

---

Hull 0   Hunslet 14

Hunslet and Hull together boasted some of the finest players in the Northern Union. The sides are pictured together prior to a match in the 1911/12 season.

method. It is indeed a pleasure to watch a footballer who relies on his brains rather than on mere speed and muscle, and Albert once more stood out as the chief figure on the field.'

Not that Albert Goldthorpe lingered in the post-match speeches, Mr Harry Ashton, the president of the Northern Union, talking 'at such length in making the presentation that Albert was well advised to cut his own remarks short, and allow his shivering colleagues to seek the shelter of the dressing room'. Not, however, before sympathising with Harry Taylor who, saying 'well, here's luck, Albert', broke his teetotal rule to drink from the champagne-filled cup.'

Flaneur reflected: 'Hunslet's success is a tribute to local ability, to the worth of men who work honestly and steadily for their living, and who have sufficient intelligence to realise that while football may be a means of increasing their income, it should never be regarded as a profession.

'It only (!) now remains for Hunslet to beat Oldham in the Northern League deciding game at Salford this weekend to complete a season that will not easily be equalled by any club in the future. There is no team one would rather see champions of Rugby football than the gallant men of Hunslet. The Northern Union Cup will have no more worthy names engraved on it than those of Albert Goldthorpe and the Hunslet club.'

Those sentiments will have been echoed by the majority of the near-20,000 throng that gathered in City Square and along Boar Lane when the Parksiders' train arrived in Leeds. Albert Goldthorpe was carried aloft by delighted supporters while a band played *See the Conquering Hero Comes* and *We've Swept the Seas Before Boys*. The *Leeds Mercury* reported: 'The people sang and shouted themselves hoarse as the team and officials drove away through the principal thoroughfares, and so down to Hunslet, where there were further rejoicings.'

Hull: Taylor, Parry, Cottrell, Cook, Rogers, Wallace, Anderson, Herridge, Owen, Carroll, Kilburn, Fulton, Holder.

Hunslet: Place, Farrar, Eagers, W. Goldthorpe, Batten, Smith, A.E. Goldthorpe, Wilson, Brookes, Jukes, Randall, Higson, Walsh.

HUNSLET v. OLDHAM

Date: 2 May 1908
Location: Salford

Championship final
Referee: Mr R. Robinson (Bradford)

Hunslet entered what had been anticipated as their final game of the 1907/8 season on the cusp of greatness. The unthinkable was now a possibility but the Parksiders could not have faced tougher opposition. It has often been stated that if Hunslet had not won all four cups in 1907/08, then the Roughyeds would have done, and the facts tend to sustain that view. Oldham, after all, won the Lancashire Cup, and came top of the Lancashire League, to emulate Hunslet in the localised competitions. The men from the Watersheddings did not, admittedly, progress too far in the Challenge Cup; but their exit, in the second round, had been at the hands of Hunslet. Moreover, Oldham had topped the league table with 28 victories and 2 draws from their 32 fixtures. Hunslet won 25 and drew 1 in a record marred by a bizarre 5 successive defeats between 18 January and 8 February, at Hull KR, Salford, Merthyr Tydfil (bizarrely, on a Monday afternoon, just two days after the setback at Salford) and Keighley, with a home reverse at the hands of Wakefield preceding the last of those losses. Fortunately, no cup ties were played during Hunslet's loss of form, but the lapse meant that Oldham finished clear at the head of the table.

People in Oldham, naturally, felt that their side should have been hailed champions and there was support from some surprising quarters. Flaneur of the *Leeds Mercury* wrote on 20 April 1908: 'One will have a good deal of sympathy with Oldham if Hunslet should be successful in the League decider... Last season Oldham were strong candidates for both the League championship and the Cup, and just failed in both at the final hurdle. This season Oldham have a much better League record than Hunslet and have, indeed, earned the championship. It will be very hard lines for them, after leading through the whole of the season, if they lose the distinction through failure in one match.

'The present League system greatly increases interest in the tournament, but it will be very harsh on Oldham if they should be defeated in the final by a club that cannot lay claim to such a fine season's record.'

The *Leeds Mercury*, by the day of the final, had rather changed its tune, stating: 'As compared with their opponents, who have had a very easy time since they were knocked out of the Cup tournament, Hunslet are handicapped. They have been at full pressure for weeks past, and the strain must have told on even the iron frames of these gallant footballers. But, with the knowledge that this is the last fence, so to speak, I fancy Hunslet will be capable of a great and worthy effort, and that a fourth trophy will be landed for Parkside.'

In the event, Oldham came very close to denying Hunslet in a game played in conditions at the furthest extreme from the previous week, when the Challenge Cup had been won in a snowstorm. Lengthy after-match speeches by Northern Union officials had kept the shivering players on the pitch longer than they would have liked – and left Hunslet without winger Fred Farrar, who had succumbed to influenza. Charlie Ward stepped up in his place, while Oldham were at full strength.

Hunslet 7   Oldham 7

HUNSLET v. OLDHAM

A contemporary artist's view of the game.

The Roughyeds drew first blood, scrum half White converting a penalty as Hunslet were repeatedly sanctioned for offside in the opening exchanges, but Albert Goldthorpe quickly restored parity when Oldham were penalised. Both sides were relying far too heavily on a kicking game but Hunslet full-back Herbert Place, in magnificent form, was up to the task of returning Oldham's kicks with interest. Nevertheless, Oldham retrieved the lead when White landed another penalty, but their advantage was to be short-lived. Albert Goldthorpe, ever-alert, simply picked the ball up as Roughyeds centre Dixon attempted to play the ball under pressure close to his own line, strolling over for a touchdown as easy as any he ever scored and adding the conversion to give the Parksiders a 7-4 interval lead.

Centre Billy Eagers had a glorious opportunity to seal the game for Hunslet when, early in the second half, he was fed a defence-splitting pass by Fred Smith directly under the Oldham posts. Inexplicably, however, the Cumbrian knocked on and the Roughyeds, boosted by the escape, levelled when Wright charged over from a scrummage for an unconverted try.

Northern Union officials had made no allowance for a draw, and the match closed in disarray. The *Leeds Mercury* reported: 'When the referee sounded his whistle for time, amid almost perfect silence, so different from the wild cheering that might have been anticipated had either side proved victorious, no one appeared to know exactly what to do. The players made their way to the stand, where three cups were on view, while many of the spectators – there were nearly twenty thousand round the ring – clamoured for the teams to "play it out."

'The players, however, had had quite enough of strenuous football on what was an almost perfect cricket afternoon, and it would have been positive cruelty to have asked them to play extra time.'

The replay was set for the following Saturday, at Belle Vue, Wakefield. Hunslet's 'All Four Cups' dream was still alive.

Hunslet: Place, C. Ward, W. Goldthorpe, Eagers, Batten, Smith, A.E. Goldthorpe, Wilson, Brookes, Jukes, Randall, Higson, Walsh.

Oldham: R. Thomas, G. Smith, Dixon, Llewellyn, Tyson, Benyon, White, Ferguson, A. Smith, Avery, Wilkinson, Wright, Longworth.

Hunslet v. Oldham

Date: 9 May 1908
Location: Belle Vue, Wakefield

Championship final replay
Referee: Mr E. Tonge (Swinton)

Hunslet duly completed the incredible feat of winning all four cups with a richly merited victory that ensured that the Championship was added to the Challenge Cup, the Yorkshire Cup and the Yorkshire League. A new record crowd at Belle Vue had been anticipated for the Championship final replay. An attendance of 23,000 had been recorded for the Challenge Cup semi-final in 1904 between Hunslet and Halifax, and the *Leeds Mercury* reported of the more recent event: 'Very early in the afternoon football enthusiasts began to roll into the "Merrie Citie" and, judging by the large number of people wearing the colours of the Parkside club, there must have been very few people left in Hunslet. There were waggonettes and cycles galore and in addition to this, heavily laden tram-cars were run from Hunslet.'

The *Mercury*, however, added that the crowd was only 'about 15,000' and pointed out: 'The difference is that in the first match the admission was sixpence, but on this occasion it was a shilling, and this fact, judging from the grumbling which one heard during the week, accounted for the comparative smallness of the attendance of locals.'

Both sides were almost unchanged, with Hunslet replacing the heavyweight sixteen-stones forward Billy Brookes with John Smales and Fred Farrar – now recovered from flu – on the wing in place of Charlie Ward. Oldham opted for Arthur Oldershaw on the wing in preference for New Zealander George Smith.

With so much at stake, it was perhaps not surprising that the match lacked something as an entertainment. The *Mercury* recorded: 'There were none of those attractive movements which the public now expect, and interesting running and passing were as rare as the visits of angels. It was a case of kicking and trusting to Providence. The passing was often injudicious and there was only one man who kicked with judgment.'

That man was, of course, Albert Goldthorpe – 'Hunslet's guide, philosopher and friend' – who steered his side to a merited victory that elevated each player to the level of legend. It was 'Ahr Albert' who put the Parksiders ahead with the first of his two goals that helped him establish a new Northern Union record of 101 goals in a season. Goldthorpe's success, scored from long range, could have been said to be against the run of play. Oldham had already had four shots at goal, with Hunslet regularly being penalised for offside, and each was missed by Joe Ferguson. Ferguson had another failure after Goldthorpe's opener, and his teammate Tom White had no better luck when he took over. The fates appeared to be conspiring towards the Parksiders, and that feeling was reinforced with a try, scored out of nothing, shortly before half-time.

Oldham were in little danger when George Tyson was tackled in his own half but the centre fared little better than his co-centre Billy Dixon had the previous week, Tyson losing the ball and Walter Goldthorpe, as alert as his brother Albert had been seven days earlier, hacked the

Hunslet 12   Oldham 2

New Zealand winger George Smith (far right), also a celebrated athlete and jockey, is pictured with, from left to right, J.C. Gleeson, J.H. Smith, Dally Messenger and 'Bumper' Wright. His talents, however, were not enough to thwart Hunslet, and he was an absentee in the Championship final replay.

ball on towards the Roughyeds try line and, with no defenders within range, touched down near the posts. Albert, unaccountably, missed the simple conversion but Hunslet were seven points ahead and had one hand on the Championship trophy as the teams withdrew for half-time.

That grip was loosened somewhat, early in the second half, when White at last got Oldham off the mark with a penalty. The Lancastrians, indeed, appeared to be on course to forcing their way back into contention when David Beynon nipped over in the corner. The scrum half had, however, stepped into touch on the way and the try was overruled. That proved to be Oldham's last hurrah. Intense pressure, repelled in the main by the wonderful Herbert Place at full-back, came to nothing and, having ridden the storm, Hunslet resumed their territorial dominance. Place dropped a goal after Fred Smith and Billy Eagers had both been thwarted in try-scoring attempts by White, and Jack Randall was halted inches short by desperate Oldham defence after Smith had charged through and his forwards had supported with a rush. Tiring Oldham, however, could do little to prevent a bout of glorious football that sealed history for Hunslet.

Billy Batten pulled the cover across with one of his typical barnstorming runs and, with the Roughyeds' rearguard in some disarray, the ball was spread wide through Eagers and Smith to Walter Goldthorpe, who crossed for a magnificent try worthy of champions. Albert, again, was unable to add the extras but the task in hand had been completed. Hunslet had achieved the impossible, with all the major trophies now in their possession, and Albert Goldthorpe, in receiving the cup from Mrs Cooke, the wife of Yorkshire County president J.B. Cooke, unsurprisingly told the crowd that the moment was 'without doubt the proudest of my life.'

Meanwhile, the feeling across the Pennines was that Oldham had hindered their own cause with their selection policy. Grasshopper, of the *Oldham Evening Chronicle*, wrote: 'Of course, the [Oldham] committee would not like the idea of dropping Beynon after his good work throughout the season, and there is no doubt that he is a very smart and clever player; but he did not come off against the burly and wily Hunslet captain. He was too small.

'That opinion was not only mine. All through the week one heard it amongst regular followers of the team. It was shared by at least some of the players, and I am informed that it was held by one

HUNSLET v. OLDHAM

ALBERT GOLDTHORPE.
HUNSLET CUPS 1907·8

Left: The greatest moment in Hunslet's history. Captain Albert Goldthorpe poses with all four cups.

Opposite page, left: The men who secured everlasting glory for Hunslet are immortalised.

Opposite page, right: None prouder. The only man to perform the 'All Four Cups' feat twice, John Willie Higson, renews acquaintance with the prize silverware, this time in the possession of Huddersfield, in 1915.

half the members of the committee and that when the team was selected on Thursday the voting was a tie on this question. There was a considerable feeling that Billy Dixon should partner White and that Birdie Dixon should be played at centre. This would probably have been a more effective combination than the one which was selected.'

Hunslet's team and officials left Belle Vue for tea at the Strafford Arms Hotel, in Wakefield, returning home to Leeds by train where, as a fortnight earlier when they had secured the Challenge Cup, they were met by a huge crowd of well wishers. There, the side transferred to an open carriage drawn by four horses. And, with all four cups proudly – so proudly – on display, the conquering heroes returned to Parkside, in all their glory, to chorus after resounding chorus of *We've Swept the Seas Before Boys*.

And so they had, founded on a fine blend of a magnificent pack, superb backs and exceptional leadership. The *Leeds Mercury's* Flaneur wrote of the great side: 'Hunslet always appear to have had magnificent forwards. The breed has not become extinct, and today we find the successors of the famous front rankers of the past labelled the "Terrible Six." The Hunslet management always seem to know where to look for forwards. Out in the colliery districts they catch them young, train them by association with the older hands, and produce year after year the finest pack in the Northern Union.

'There have been famous packs at Halifax, Leeds, Warrington, Wigan, Oldham and Salford, but for downright consistency over a long period of years commend me to Hunslet.

'Fortunately at the present time the backs are well worthy of the forwards. A few years ago I used to go down to Parkside and watch the great-hearted pack, which included Shooter and Glow, Harry Wilson and other famous players, tearing themselves to pieces week after week, only to be shockingly let down by a back division that, apart from the Goldthorpes, had little idea of the art of back play.

'All this is now changed. Albert Goldthorpe is assisted at half back by one of the sturdiest and smartest halves in the North, Fred Smith, while at three-quarters Eagers is a much finer and more "brainy" player than in his best Bradford days, and Farrar and Batten are wings with speed, resource, and a thorough knowledge of the game. Walter Goldthorpe has shown much improved form in the later part of the season, and fits well into the scheme of things, while, as to Place at full-back, I would rather have in on my side than any other custodian in Yorkshire save Harry Taylor.

'Place has learnt a lesson in self-control, and in keeping his temper he has improved his game. He is not such a great kicker as Little or Gunn, but his punts have quite length enough, and he is both a fine field and a strong tackler. I would pit Hunslet against the rest of the Northern Union at Parkside, and look confidently on them to win.'

Hunslet: Place, Farrar, Eagers, W. Goldthorpe, Batten, A.E. Goldthorpe, Smith, Wilson, Jukes, Randall, Higson, Walsh, Smales.

Oldham: R. Thomas, Tyson, Dixon, Llewellyn, Oldershaw, White, Benyon, Ferguson, A. Smith, Avery, Wilkinson, Wright, Longworth.

Hunslet v. Leeds

Date: 31 March 1909
Location: Parkside

Challenge Cup second round
Referee: Mr W. McCutcheon (Oldham)

Hunslet's pre-eminence over their neighbours from north of the river continued with a comfortable victory, maintaining a trend dating back to before the launch of the Northern Union. Leeds' role of underdogs against their illustrious rivals had been remarked on at the turn of the year when the *Athletic News*, reflecting on the Parksiders' 21-5 win over the Loiners on Boxing Day before a 14,000 crowd, asserted: 'Twenty years and more ago it used to be said that the sight of a Wakefield Trinity jersey used to palsy the nerves of the Bradford team. Must not something of the same kind be said now of the Hunslet jersey and the Leeds club's representatives? If ever a team appeared likely to win "hands down" it was the Leeds thirteen in the return match with Hunslet on Saturday. The previous day Hunslet had been thrashed by Halifax by 31 points, whereas Leeds had won the honours, if not the score, in the match with the Australians and, in addition, had secured ten league points within a month in five successive matches. Yet Hunslet won the league game by 21 points to 5. Albert Goldthorpe had been "dug out" once again, and showed that he can still kick goals, if he cannot reproduce his old smartness in other directions.'

The *News* continued: 'It is instructive to note that since the formation of the Northern Union Hunslet and Leeds have, up to and including last Saturday's engagement, met in 29 league and cup matches, and that Hunslet have won 20 games and Leeds 7, the other two having been draws. The Hunslet score in that series of matches amounts to 271 points, and Leeds' to 160. The testimony to the superiority of Hunslet which these figures convey is unmistakable.'

That ascendancy continued when the teams met again the following spring. The match attracted the biggest crowd to watch the 'All Four Cups' side that season, 23,000 turning up to eclipse the 20,000 that had descended on Watersheddings for the league fixture in December at Oldham. Leeds were, again, rated as underdogs for the Challenge Cup tie and Flaneur of the *Leeds Mercury* remarked: 'The superiority of Hunslet over Leeds has become a tradition. I need not wade through statistics; everyone who knows anything of Northern Union football in Leeds is well aware that Hunslet have always been the predominant partner, and that the men of Headingley have never defeated their neighbours in a cup-tie. I have tried to find a supporter of the Leeds club who is confident of his team's success today. I have not succeeded. I have tried to find a Hunslet man who regards Leeds as having, at any rate, an outside chance. Again I have failed.' Flaneur, however, had a word of caution for the Parksiders: 'Hunslet have the stronger team but Leeds, with a pull all together, with some extra special tackling, and a little bit of luck, which has not often gone their way in matches with their neighbours, are capable of establishing a precedent.'

The *Leeds Mercury's* headline, two days later, was 'Hunslet Again Outplay Leeds in a Cup Tie.' Leeds, who against all expectations had taken an early lead, withdrew into all their old anxieties and Flaneur observed: 'It seemed to me that the Leeds men were obsessed by tradition, that they

Hunslet 15   Leeds 9

The legendary Albert Goldthorpe breaks from a scrum against Leeds. Winger Fred Farrar is poised and stand-off Fred Smith, in the background, is alert to developments.

felt by the start they were battling not only against Hunslet, but against Fate, and that if the home team got in front all hope might as well be abandoned. They had chances early on but they were too anxious to accept them, and every one who has watched the course of Leeds and Hunslet battles must have felt that the game was over when Farrar got his try and Cappleman kicked his great goal from the touchline.'

So, indeed, it was. Harry Wilson, playing his first game since sustaining an injury in the Boxing Day success over the Loiners, was a colossus in leading the pack, Flaneur enthusing: 'He stands in a class by himself. He got a nasty cut over the eye in the first half, but this was no matter to him, and his play throughout was magnificent. Harry Wilson is still easily the best forward in the Northern Union; you can look where you like for the next.' Walter Goldthorpe, meanwhile, excelled in the Leeds cause, having transferred to Headingley earlier in the campaign. The veteran, though, may well have pondered on the wisdom of his move as Hunslet added tries by Tom Walsh and Billy Eagers to Farrar's early touchdown, with Cappleman and Goldthorpe each kicking a drop goal.

Leeds had the last word, as the Parksiders eased off, when winger Desborough crossed for their only try; full-back Young kicked three goals for a side that, once again, found itself outclassed by the men from south Leeds. Hunslet, however, were about to experience a downwards spiral that would span two decades.

Hunslet: Cappleman, Farrar, Eagers, Hoyle, Batten, Smith, A.E. Goldthorpe, Higson, Wilson, Walsh, Brookes, Randall, Jukes.

Leeds: Young, Desborough, Ware, W. Goldthorpe, Fawcett, Ward, Jones, Webster, Harrison, Whitaker, Townend, Wainwright, Birch.

Hull Kingston Rovers v. Hunslet

Date: 30 November 1929
Location: Headingley, Leeds

Yorkshire Cup final
Referee: Mr F. Fairhurst (Wigan)

Hunslet's first appearance in a major final for over twenty years ended in defeat, but with hindsight the result was of secondary importance. After two decades in the doldrums the portents were clear; the Parksiders, while unlikely ever to regain their former standing as 'All Four Cups' winners – an achievement beyond the wildest dreams of all but the most irrational supporter of any club – were clearly about to become a force again. Significantly, the prime movers in this slow but solid transformation were the supporters themselves.

Seven years earlier, with the club at its lowest ebb after having finished fourth from bottom of the table as the 1920s arrived, the supporters' association was formed and that initiative, and the practical and sustained contributions of that body, resulted in gradual strengthening of the team. Made famous as the 'jam jar' club, with vital funds raised from that source that kept Hunslet alive, the Parksiders were able to recruit players in the early part of the decade of the calibre of Frank 'Dolly' Dawson, while Hector Crowther had put pen to paper in 1919 and the immortal Walter Guerin was already on the books. Others to arrive as Hunslet assembled a more-than-capable side included the likes of the fearsome Harry Beverley, who initially played in the centre but would become best known as a rampaging yet cultured second row forward, and winger George Broughton. Others who would also make their mark included prop Jim Traill, stand-off George Todd and hooker Les White.

Arguably the greatest figure to join the club was Jack Walkington, a young full-back enticed from Burley RUFC in March 1927. Walkington would give wonderful service to Hunslet as a player and coach for the next thirty-three years before continuing as a director. The future captain joined a side that had already begun a climb up the rankings, rising to fourth in 1927/28 before losing 12-2 in the championship semi-final to eventual 'All Four Cups' winners Swinton. After a further year of consolidation, Hunslet progressed to the 1929 Yorkshire Cup final the hard way, with each of their three ties being played away from home. Leeds, themselves now a force after having been little more than fodder for the Parksiders in the days of the Northern Union, were accounted for 11-5 at Headingley, and that win was followed by an 8-4 verdict at the Boulevard against Hull. The final hurdle of Keighley was circumvented 3-0 at Lawkholme Lane, securing a tilt against Hull Kingston Rovers in the final at Headingley.

Hunslet, who had changed their strip that season to white shirts with a broad chocolate band, were rated as underdogs against a side that had twice won the championship during the decade, and their prospects weren't helped by the fact that they were without regular hooker Les White. The Parksiders switched Henry Moss from the second row and the stand in certainly did his job, 'getting the ball well' according to Arthur Bostock of the *Leeds Mercury*.

Hunslet, however, never recovered from a dreadful start in which Rovers scored within the first thirty seconds to stun the 12,000 crowd. Walkington appeared to be out of position when Hull

---

Hull KR 13   Hunslet 7

The appearance in the Yorkshire Cup final, followed within a month by the victory over Australia, confirmed that Hunslet were re-emerging as a force. Within two seasons the Parksiders would secure some silverware to prove it. The 1931/32 side is pictured with the Yorkshire League Championship cup.

essayed an early kick and Beverley, chasing back, slipped on the greasy turf, Harry 'Scrubber' Dale scoring for Rovers in a subsequent 'rush.' Kingston Rovers went on to have much the better of the first half against a reeling Hunslet side. Rainton crossed the Parksiders' goal line, Jack Spamer followed suit, and Laurie Osborne kicked two goals to establish a 13-2 interval lead, with the Parksiders limited to a penalty by Traill.

Hunslet, however, 'won' the second half. The Robins were denied any further score, while prop Dai Jenkins forced his way in for a try that was allowed despite an element of doubt as to its validity. Traill added the extras but it wasn't enough in a game in which half-backs George Todd and Billy Thornton were felt to have utilised the short kick too often, dangerous winger George Broughton being starved of quality possession as a result.

Former Hunslet star Billy Gilston lamented afterwards that the Parksiders' forwards should have sought to progress by wheeling the scrummage. The *Mercury's* Bostock, however, wrote: 'He had to confess that wheeling the pack is a lost art in these degenerate days. In Mr Gilston's time the Parkside forwards, like those at Batley, were adept at this phase of the game. They used to take the ball with them. It was more effective than the eternal scrape, scrape, scrape.'

Hull KR: Osborne, Bateman, Cook, Jordan, Rainton, Dale, Spamer, Britton, Sharpe, Roberts, Binks, Westerdale, Williams.

Hunslet: Walkington, Rhodes, Coulson, Beverley, Broughton, Todd, Thornton, Jenkins, Moss, Traill, Dawson, Crowther, Chapman.

HUNSLET v. AUSTRALIA

Date: 25 December 1929   Tour match
Location: Parkside

Harry Jepson, who was assistant secretary and then secretary of Hunslet from the mid-1950s until the early 1970s, recounts how, during a lunch with former players in Australia, he let slip where he came from. 'Hunslet!' exploded one of his hosts. 'That God-forsaken place! I've been there; never again. It's a grimy Hell on Earth!' Stunned, Jepson said little in reply, until it turned out that his new friend's only experience of the suburb had been on the 1929 Australian tour of England.

'Oh, that explains why you didn't like it,' said Harry. 'If I remember rightly' (which of course he did) 'you lost that game, didn't you? And wasn't it played on Christmas Day, when perhaps you'd have rather been elsewhere, perhaps on the other side of the world with your families?' The Aussie – in common with so many others in debate with Harry Jepson – was obliged to concede, which is something Hunslet assuredly did not do against a Kangaroos party that would lose just one more game on that trip. Australia, who had won the First Test at Hull KR before going down in the Second Test at Leeds, would make history by playing an unprecedented and never-to-be-repeated four Tests. The Kangaroos, after losing to Hunslet, beat Hull KR and had their game at Wigan abandoned, after having been 10-9 in front, before drawing the Third Test at Swinton 0-0. That result, though, was shrouded in controversy when Australian half-back Chimpy Busch had a 'try' disallowed in the closing seconds after being tackled into touch by Swinton loose forward Fred Butters while diving over. Great Britain won the hastily arranged Fourth Test 3-0 but Hunslet had enjoyed the biggest victory of the tour, the fifteen-point margin bettering successes by Wakefield (14-3), Leeds (8-7), Swinton (9-5) Northern League (18-5), Cumberland (8-5) and Warrington (17-8).

In a game redolent of the days of the 'Terrible Six', the Parksiders owed their success to a strong performance by their forwards who followed a precipitant lead set by the backs. A 12,000 gate, the second best of the season after the 20,000 that witnessed the 12-12 draw with Leeds in September, saw Hunslet take control on a pitch that, after heavy rain, was in deplorable condition, with pools of water lying on the surface and a strong wind further hindering play. Stand-off George Todd, criticised only a month earlier for kicking too often in the Yorkshire Cup final defeat at the hands of Hull KR, earned plaudits on this occasion for adopting the same approach. His forwards, the *Leeds Mercury* reported, 'rallied to support them, and the result was that the Tourists were given as stiff a gruelling as they have had on the tour.' A sequence of forward rushes kept the Kangaroos under the cosh and Australia's option of moving the ball failed to trouble an uncompromising defence.

The result, given the conditions, was never in doubt once Hunslet, despite playing against the wind, took the lead with a converted try by winger George Broughton, who would close the season with 31 touchdowns. The Parksiders, ahead 5-0 at the break, declined to rest on their laurels and the

---

Hunslet 18   Australia 3

Cumbrian Billy Hannah, who joined Hunslet from Maryport, played in the Parksiders' first game in the Northern Union. Hannah subsequently became Hunslet's trainer, ensuring the team's peak fitness for the 'All Four Cups' glory of 1907/08 and continuing in that role through the testing decades of the 1910s and 1920s and into the sunshine of the 1930s. Hannah is pictured in August 1934 giving a pep talk to Harry Beverley and Dolly Dawson, two of the heroes of the win over Australia, and (centre) Harry Goulthorpe.

tourists' desperate bid to rescue the situation by switching Bill Shankland to the centre, with Paddy Maher moving out to the wing, failed to come off. Hector Crowther and Dai Jenkins continued to dominate up front and Todd and full-back Jack Walkington offered grand support in the backs. With the tourists 'driven to kick the ball oftener than they have done in any previous match' the Parksiders duly added tries by Todd, centre Johnny Coulson and loose forward George Chapman, while Walkington and Jim Traill finished with three and two goals respectively.

The *Mercury* reflected: 'There was no questioning the merit of Hunslet's victory, and the "gate" of £850 was highly satisfactory in view of the conditions.' The result remains Hunslet's only win over an Australian touring side. The Kangaroos had pipped the Parksiders 12-11 in their first trip to England, in 1908/09, and drew 3-3 two years later. Hunslet slipped 19-10 in 1921/22, gained revenge in 1929, and were then hammered 49-2 in 1952. That result was improved upon four years later, with a 27-11 defeat, and the Parksiders were beaten by the odd point in 23 in 1959 before playing their final game against Australia in 1963, when the tourists prevailed 17-13.

Hunslet, however, have fared rather better against New Zealand. The pioneering tourists of 1907/08 were held to an 11-11 draw, the 1926/27 party were beaten 13-12, and the first post-war Kiwis of 1947/48 were disposed of 18-10. The Parksiders, in fact, have never lost to New Zealand, the nearest approximation to a defeat being in 1961 when a Leeds XIII, made up of players from Bramley, Hunslet and Leeds, succumbed 24-9 at Headingley.

Hunslet: Walkington, Rhodes, Coulson, Beverley, Broughton, Todd, Thornton, Jenkins, White, Traill, Dawson, Crowther, Chapman.

Australia: McMillan, Shankland, Fifield, Maher, Upton, Edwards, Laws, Kingston, Sellars, Root, Steinohrt, Henderson, Dempsey.

Hunslet v. Widnes

Date: 5 May 1934   **Challenge Cup final**
Location: Wembley Stadium, London   **Referee:** Mr A. Holbrook (Warrington)

Lord Derby, the president of the Rugby Football League, became the first 'substitute' in a Challenge Cup final – thirty-one years before the rule allowing replacements was introduced – when he stepped forward at short notice as guest of honour in place of King George V. His Majesty, whose son the Prince of Wales had presented the Challenge Cup to Huddersfield twelve months earlier when the Fartowners overcame Warrington, was unable to attend because of continued ill health and Lord Derby was a more-than-willing replacement.

Hunslet, unfortunately, were unable to call on a stand-in when Cyril Morrell was injured in the twenty-sixth minute. The centre fractured his collarbone in the act of scoring the Parksiders' first try, two Widnes defenders effecting a last-ditch tackle that could not deny Morrell his touchdown but which was to bring his involvement in the match to a premature close. Morrell, after departing the fray with suspected shoulder bruising, quickly returned to action but it soon became apparent that his condition was serious enough to warrant his permanent withdrawal. That left Hunslet, 5-3 ahead, facing the remainder of the game with only twelve men against a Widnes side that had staged a massive upset four years earlier with a 10-3 win against a star-studded St Helens. The Chemics, in 1930, had fielded twelve local men in their line-up. On this occasion their entire team hailed from Widnes but the strong bond engendered by that fact – and previous Wembley experience in the shape of prop Nat Silcock (now elevated to captain), centre Peter Topping, winger Harry Owen, Albert Ratcliffe (in the second row after appearing in the centre in 1930) and Harry Millington, now at loose forward from the second row – wasn't enough to deny Hunslet, who had nine south Leeds lads in their side.

With Harry Beverley, a former centre, switched from loose forward to cover for the absent Morrell, the Parksiders were able to accomplish what they hadn't been able to manage with a full complement; deny Widnes a try. The Chemics had opened their account after only five minutes when second row Hugh McDowell crashed over, Hunslet responding with a penalty for prop Mark Tolson with what would turn out to be his only success of the afternoon. Jack Walkington's ploy, after winning the toss, of electing to play with his back to the strong sun paid dividends in terms of territorial advantage, Walkington's astute kicks from full-back posing problems for the Chemics' beleaguered defence.

Walkington, in his first season as captain after having taken over the mantle from Hector Crowther, also brought his handling skills to bear to fine effect in Hunslet's first try. The skipper, with left centre Ernest Winter, prised out an opening in Widnes' defence and Morrell did the rest. Widnes were all too aware of the threat of winger George Dennis, who had created a new club record in the 57-2 league victory over Bradford in January with seven tries. Cleverly deluding the Chemics with a series of dummies to his foil, Morrell held off several defenders to crash over for a sensational score that, sadly,

---

Hunslet 11   Widnes 5

Safely back home at Parkside, the team enjoys posing with the Challenge Cup.

was also to herald his exit from the Wembley stage. Hunslet held out for the remainder of the half but the portents didn't look too good when Widnes opened the second period with a penalty, after only two minutes, for Ratcliffe. That goal levelled the scores and, with Widnes applying heavy pressure, ambitions of retrieving the Challenge Cup after a gap of twenty-six years appeared to be slim. No one, however, had told the Hunslet players who, to a man, rose to the challenge against a side that had finished just one place below them – seventh to the Parksiders' sixth – in the league table.

With their supporters in the 41,280 crowd (only 600 less than in the previous year, when glamour sides Huddersfield and Warrington had clashed) providing rousing support, the Parksiders held firm and duly weathered the storm. Having thwarted Widnes, Hunslet successfully turned defence into attack. Second row pair Frank 'Dolly' Dawson and Crowther began to make significant inroads into the Lancastrians' defence and it was Dawson's break direct from a scrum that led to Beverley going over. Tolson's miss, however, left the Parksiders only three points ahead but, try as they may, Widnes were unable to break the courageous twelve-man Hunslet defence.

The Parksiders, deservedly, finished the stronger and sealed a magnificent victory when stand-off George Todd and Dawson – who would surely have been a serious contender for the Lance Todd Trophy had that award been in existence at the time – combined for prop Len Smith to crash over for a try that delighted not only supporting winger George Broughton but also ball boy Syd Rookes, who was to sign for Hunslet towards the end of the decade for a huge £120 after having negotiated an increase from the original offer of £20. Another boy on the sidelines who was equally enthralled was Harry Jepson, down for the final at only ten years of age. Jepson, who went on to become secretary at Hunslet and then chairman, and subsequently president, of Leeds, recalls: 'It

Hunslet v. Widnes

To the soiled, the spoils! A tired but elated Jack Walkington shows off the Challenge Cup in the Wembley dressing rooms.

was wonderful, simply wonderful. Jack Walkington came towards the boys' pen after having been presented with the Challenge Cup by Lord Derby. I reached out and I touched his jersey. I always remember when I got home, telling my mother, "Mam, I touched Jack Walkington's jersey."'

It was a fine day, too, for Hunslet chairman Jim Lewthwaite. Lewthwaite was to return to Wembley, as Rugby League chairman, twelve months later to present the cup to Castleford, who ironically beat Hunslet, before 25,000 fans – still a record at Wheldon Road – in the quarter-final. Lewthwaite, a Cumbrian who had joined Hunslet as a player, had a fellow countyman to thank for his involvement in the Parksiders' success, trainer Billy Hannah – another strong link with the past, having also played for the club at the turn of the century in addition to having coached the 'All Four Cups' side of 1907/08 – also having travelled down from the far North-West. Neither man had enjoyed a stress-free route to the final. Hunslet's Challenge Cup record over the previous decade had been lamentable, with only one quarter-final appearance (at eventual finalists St Helens, in 1930), but that sorry litany was assuaged with a series of hard-fought victories. Leigh, struggling in the lower reaches of the table, proved a tough nut to crack in the first round before the Parksiders returned from Hilton Park with an 8-6 verdict. It was just as difficult, more so in fact, at the next stage against Castleford. Walkington and his charges forced a 4-4 draw with only twelve men after centre Ernest Winter was injured, and the Parksiders were indeed reduced to eleven players at once stage when Dawson also had to be withdrawn. Hunslet, however, held out before a 23,000 crowd and eased to the delight of their supporters in the 19,000 'gate' at Parkside eased through the replay 23-0. Widnes, meanwhile, were progressing relatively comfortably, registering a 12-3 home win over Leeds and a 10-0 victory at Hull KR.

A young supporter shares the moment with Hunslet captain Jack Walkington and Frank 'Dolly' Dawson as the Parksiders are feted on their return to Leeds.

Hunslet are introduced to the chief guest, Lord Derby.

Wembley fever began to mount in both camps as the quarter-finals beckoned, and both eventual finalists were tested before reaching the penultimate stage. Widnes won 5-3 at Halifax while Hunslet were facing a similarly difficult fixture with the visit of a York outfit that was to finish fifth in the table. A solitary Tolson goal was enough to see the Parksiders through in a rousing encounter before a 13,590 crowd, but Hunslet had ridden their luck, York having what the Minstermen reckoned was a perfectly good try disallowed. Huddersfield, the holders, were now the only remaining barrier to Hunslet's bid, while Widnes contemplated the prospect of Oldham as a cross-county final beckoned. The Chemics duly prevailed 7-4, while 27,450 baying fans witnessed a fine 12-7 victory for the Parksiders at Belle Vue, Wakefield. Harry Goulthorpe and Dennis grabbed the tries, Tolson kicking three goals, in a game in which Hunslet had led 5-0 at half-time. There was, however, gloom for prop Jim Traill, who was injured in the win over York and, despite returning to action, was unable to force his way into the Wembley line-up. Traill's turn was to come with Keighley in 1937 – ironically against Widnes – while his son Ken was to earn Wembley glory as a player with Bradford Northern in the late 1940s and, as a coach, with the great Wakefield Trinity sides of the 1960s.

Hunslet: Walkington, Dennis, Morrell, Winter, Broughton, Todd, Thornton, Tolson, White, Smith, Crowther, Dawson, Beverley.

Widnes: Bradley, Owen, Topping, Jacks, Gallimore, Shannon, McCue, Silcock, Jones, Higgins, McDowell, Ratcliffe, Millington.

HUNSLET v. BARROW

Date: 23 April 1938   Championship semi-final
Location: Parkside   **Referee:** Mr G.S. Phillips (Widnes)

Hunslet, in their Jubilee year at Parkside and in what was also Jack Walkington's and 'Dolly' Dawson's benefit season, fittingly achieved something that had been beyond any of their predecessors, even the fabulous 'All Four Cups' side of thirty years before. The Parksiders, for the first time, finished the league campaign on top of the table and as such were obvious favourites to secure the championship, which was determined by the means of a play-off involving the leading four teams.

As the side in pole position, Hunslet were given a home pairing with fourth-placed Barrow; and it was lost on no one that with Leeds (second) hosting third-placed Swinton, a derby final was a real possibility. Hunslet headed the rankings despite an indifferent start to the season in which five of the first nine league games had ended in defeat. That uncertain opening, however, was largely forgotten as the side recorded seven victories on the trot between the 23-12 home win over Batley on 23 October and the 13-3 verdict against Oldham at Parkside in mid-December. A defeat at Castleford and successive draws against York and Wakefield put something of a dampener on the Christmas festivities but the rest of the campaign was to prove hugely successful on the league front. The Parksiders repeated their previous seven-match winning run, culminating in a 14-10 victory over Dewsbury on 12 February in the designated Jubilee match, played before a 10,000 crowd.

Hunslet travelled to Liverpool Stanley the following week in the first round of the Challenge Cup reasonably confident of success against a side that was to finish seventeenth in the table. In the event, the Parksiders returned to Leeds reflecting on a 6-5 defeat, despite a fine try by Eric Batten that thrilled the away fans in the 4,647 crowd. But, as many championship-winning sides have discovered over the years, an early exit from the Challenge Cup can be of value on other fronts. Walkington's men, after losing at Barrow in the next game and going down at Hull following a home win over Keighley, recovered their poise to stay unbeaten throughout the rest of the domestic season. That heady sequence set up the return to south Leeds of Barrow, who had been edged 2-0, courtesy of a Mark Tolson goal, before 12,000 spectators in the home fixture in mid-March.

On this occasion 16,000 gathered at Parkside, most in anticipation of a Hunslet win, and they were not to be disappointed. Barrow, scheduled to play at Wembley a fortnight later, had a slightly jaded look about them after a punishing schedule of nine matches in fifteen days, but that did not detract from a Hunslet display that, according to Hugh Whitfield of the *Leeds Mercury*, abounded with zest and hunger.

No one typified that more than scrum half Willie Thornton, who Whitfield described as 'a compact parcel of all the Hunslet football virtues, full of enthusiasm, enterprise and will to win.

Hunslet 13   Barrow 7

Jack Walkington enjoyed a well-deserved benefit in 1937/38. The centrepiece was a fixture against a Vic Hey XIII. The Hunslet skipper shakes hands with his Leeds counterpart, watched by gifted Welsh stand-off Oliver Morris (far left) and another great son of the Valleys in Alex Givvons (far right).

'A team with that "tired feeling" will never get the better of these Hunslet enthusiasts, whose play was as enlivening as a whiff of Blackpool air and a glass of champagne combined.'

The reporter enthused: 'Perhaps he overdid the kicking, but he also threw out some of those astonishingly long passes that startle opposing defences. In defence he was superb, falling back with fine judgment. Hunslet had two full-backs. One was called Walkington; the other, Thornton.'

All three of Hunslet's touchdowns were 'snap' tries, arising from kicks rather than passing movements. The Parksiders established an 8-2 interval lead through the first two, centre Frank Yates netting the opener after charging down a clearance and winger Eric Batten recording the second after centre Ernest Winter had broken the defence and kicked to the line. Walkington added a conversion but Barrow forced their way back into the issue early in the second period when stand-off Ian Lloyd scored a fine solo try, Alec Troup kicking his second goal to reduce the deficit to a single point. The Furnessmen came close to going in front when Lloyd was narrowly wide with a drop goal attempt but Hunslet's response was swift and effective. Walkington, who had generally adopted a safety first approach, opted to abjure the tactic, firing out a difficult pass that winger Jimmy O'Sullivan took with aplomb before kicking across to the Barrow posts where Winter, following up at high pace, beat a posse of defenders to a touchdown which Walkington converted.

The score knocked the stuffing out of Barrow, who would suffer even greater anguish fourteen days later in the Challenge Cup final with a 7-4 defeat at the hands of Salford when skipper Troup, collecting a loose ball near his own line, threw out a wild pass for no apparent reason that Salford centre Albert Gear collected for the crucial score. There were claims afterwards that a Red Devils player had called for the ball but Barrow could have no such complaints about the defeat at Hunslet, who had proved themselves worthy winners on the journey to confirm their status as the best side in the British game.

Hunslet: Walkington, Batten, Yates, Winter, O'Sullivan, Morris, Thornton, Tolson, White, Bennett, Newbound, Stansfield, Plenderleith.

Barrow: Johnson, Cumberbatch, Higgins, McDonnell, Thornburrow, Lloyd, Little, Rawlings, McKeating, Skelly, Troup, Greenhalgh, Marklew.

HUNSLET v. LEEDS

Date: 30 April 1938
Location: Elland Road, Leeds

Championship final
Referee: Mr F. Fairhurst (Wigan)

Prior to 1938, the record attendance for a Championship final had been the 31,564 who turned up at Wilderspool, Warrington, for the 1933/34 decider between Salford and eventual winners Wigan. Two other finals had broken the 31,000 barrier: in 1930/31, when that attendance was recorded at Swinton's win over Leeds at Wigan, and in 1936/37 when 31,500 turned up, again at Central Park, for the meeting of Salford and Warrington. A similar crowd was expected when Hunslet, Leeds, Swinton and Barrow qualified for the 1937/38 top-four play-offs and Rugby Football League bosses saw no initial reason to break from the precedent of using Rugby League venues for one of the sport's great showpiece occasions. Belle Vue, the home of Wakefield Trinity and only a matter of ten miles or so south of Leeds, was the early favourite with the game's rulers and the ground was no stranger to hosting the big occasion.

Hunslet had completed their 'All Four Cups' feat of 1907/08 on that very stage, beating Oldham 12-2 in the Championship final replay before a 14,054 crowd, and Belle Vue subsequently hosted four more Championship deciders. Seventeen thousand witnessed Huddersfield's 29-2 romp over Wigan in 1912/13, and two years later Huddersfield's 'Team of All the Talents' secured their own 'All Four Cups' legacy with a 35-2 verdict against Leeds in front of 14,000.

A gate of 30,350 gathered for the 2-2 draw involving Huddersfield and Leeds in 1929/30, and 19,386 amassed for the meeting of Huddersfield and eventual champions St Helens in 1931/32. Wakefield had also played host to 29,335 supporters when Leeds beat Hull 28-3 in the 1922/23 Challenge Cup final, and Belle Vue was favoured for Challenge Cup semi-finals in 1931/32 (21,000 being attracted for the replay between Leeds and Halifax), 1932/33 (a crowd of 36,359, when Huddersfield overcame Leeds), 1933/34 – Hunslet reaching Wembley for the first time, 27,450 thrilling to a 12-7 success over Huddersfield – and in 1935/36 when Leeds secured their second appearance at the Empire Stadium with a 10-5 win against Huddersfield before 37,906. With several Yorkshire Cup finals completing the curriculum vitae, Wakefield had a proven track record. And neither Hunslet or Leeds could disparage the qualities of the stadium.

It quickly became clear, however, that interest in a potential final involving Hunslet and Leeds was reaching fever-pitch proportions in the city and that Wakefield's ability to accommodate what could clearly be a record crowd for rugby league, putting the previous best of 51,250 for the 1936 Challenge Cup final between Leeds and Warrington in danger, had to be questioned. Passions had become inflamed even before the finalists had been verified. With leaders Hunslet – celebrating fifty years at Parkside – hosting fourth-placed Barrow and Leeds (second) entertaining Swinton, the prospect of the derby-to-end-all-derbies becoming a reality was obvious. There had twice been opportunities, but disappointment, in the preceding decade. In 1927/28 Hunslet and Leeds both lost their semi-finals, to Swinton and Featherstone Rovers respectively, after finishing in the top four,

Hunslet 8   Leeds 2

Leeds skipper Vic Hey congratulates captain Jack Walkington on the Parksiders' victory. Hunslet chairman Jim Lewthwaite watches anxiously as Hey gives every impression of absconding with the cup!

and it was a similar story in 1931/32 when the Parksiders slipped to Huddersfield and Leeds went down to St Helens.

With the duo now fancied to progress past the penultimate stage, however, Loiners' chairman Sir Edwin Airey became the prime mover behind the Elland Road initiative, insisting that the game should be staged in a stadium capable of housing all who wanted to be part of history, and that Leeds United's ground was the ideal and the obvious venue. Hunslet chairman Jim Lewthwaite and his committee agreed with Sir Edwin's argument that the Elland Road option also eased the financial burden, in travelling terms, on those supporters who were less well off. And on Wednesday 20 April – three days before the Parksiders hosted Barrow, and five days before the Loiners entertained Swinton – a joint deputation travelled to the Rugby Football League's headquarters at Chapeltown Road, Leeds, to present their case. However, with others insisting that the two clubs were acting prematurely in assuming they would succeed in reaching the decider, the RFL held firm, announcing Belle Vue as the stage for Saturday 30 April.

Wakefield, though, would have been a strange venue for a final between Barrow and Swinton, and perhaps even more controversial for a game involving either of the two Leeds teams against either of the Lancastrian sides. The Parksiders and the Loiners, supported by a deluge of protest from supporters and floods of letters to the local press felt confident enough to remount their proposal after Hunslet beat Barrow in the first of the semi-finals. The RFL liaised with three members who were in France with Great Britain and – with the remainder convened at Headingley following Leeds' win over Swinton – the original ruling was reversed in favour of Elland Road.

Hunslet v. Leeds

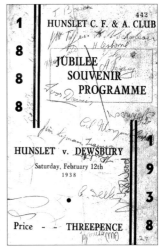

Left: Irish winger Jimmy O'Sullivan, who scored Hunslet's second try, shapes to pass. Cyril Plenderleith (in the number fourteen shirt in an era in which loose forwards sought to avoid wearing 'unlucky' thirteen) looks on.

*Right:*The 1938 championship coincided with Hunslet's Silver Jubilee year at Parkside. Dewsbury provided the opposition on the day of celebration.

In reality, the game was being staged at what, at root, was a rugby league ground. Elland Road had been the home of Holbeck, who resigned from Northern Union at the end of the 1903/04 season after losing a play-off game with St Helens to determine which team would be promoted from Division Two with leaders Wakefield Trinity. Holbeck became Leeds City AFC, who were thrown out of the Football League shortly after the First World War for alleged irregularities, Leeds United emerging from the debris. After a gap of thirty-four years, therefore, rugby posts were once again erected at Elland Road, the RFL opting to use Hunslet's rather than Leeds' taller set because of easier access and ease of erection.

The game itself hinged on the clash at stand-off between the Loiners' giant Australian, Vic Hey, who weighed in at 13st 12lbs, and the Parksiders' diminutive Welsh maestro Oliver Morris (10st 2lbs), who had come north from Pontypridd at the beginning of the season. Morris, initially likened to a 'rabbit' by his teammates because of his slight physique, quickly belied that impression with his lightning speed, sure handling and astonishing tackling. In an echo of the 1892 Yorkshire Cup final, when Leeds' stand-off Potter outweighed each member of the Hunslet pack, Morris had the better of Hey.

Hunslet, going into the game on the back of a league 'double' over the Loiners, who had lost 16-10 at Parkside and 8-5 at Headingley, went behind to an early penalty by Leeds second row Ted Tattersfield, and did well to hold their opponents out while reduced to twelve men for a spell because of an injury to Mark Tolson. The Loiners could – some observers felt should – have settled the issue in that ten-minute period but wasted a number of opportunities with poor finishing. Two chances went astray on Hunslet's exposed left flank, the first when a pass by centre Evan Williams flew over the shoulder of Australian winger Eric Harris, the Toowoomba Ghost. The Parksiders had another escape when Charlie Eaton, who had looped Harris to create an overlap, failed to hold the

Mercurial stand-off Oliver Morris. The diminutive Welshman, rated by many good judges as one of the finest players of all time, shone at Elland Road. Morris was to die serving his country in the Second World War.

final pass. And another Leeds chance went begging when Hey powered his way through only to have no one in support when halted by Hunslet full-back and captain Jack Walkington.

Walkington's men made Leeds pay for their profligacy with two tries in five minutes that ultimately retrieved the championship after a thirty-year gap following their 'All Four Cups' campaign. Centre Winter was the hero, grabbing the first in the twenty-third minute with a remarkable solo attack in which he left two front-line defenders floundering, disposed of another couple with a dummy and swerve and held off Dai Jenkins sufficiently in a thrilling chase to the try line to put his side ahead. And it was Winter, again, who created the second score, making inroads into Leeds' defence before delaying his pass sufficiently to entice Eric Harris before sending his Irish winger Jimmy O'Sullivan over in the corner. Winter, however, was matched by his co-centre Cyril Morrell who had a huge impact, almost scoring after a raid in which he beat half-a-dozen defenders, and commanding the Leeds three-quarters in defence.

Had the Harry Sunderland Trophy for the Man of the Match existed at the time, however, the recipient would surely have been Walkington, whose kicking in the first half, against the wind, was meticulous, and his second-half peppering of Leeds winger Stanley Smith, who had sustained a sprained ankle, portentous. Walkington added a goal to his side's cause and the Parksiders, despite conceding twelve penalties in a committed display, denied Leeds any further score. Hunslet, who had enjoyed the majority of possession in the first half, lost the scrums 3-1 in the second period as Tolson's injury had its effect. They held out though, as the Loiners also struggled with injuries. Leeds, with Hey shifted to the wing with both thigh muscles gone and Smith also hurt, rarely threatened after that strong start, leaving Hunslet deserved winners before a record attendance that, it was felt, would have been higher if stewards had packed the crowd more efficiently at the Gelderd Road end.

Hunslet: Walkington, Batten, Morrell, Winter, O'Sullivan, Morris, Thornton, Tolson, White, Bennett, Newbound, Stansfield, Plenderleith.

Leeds: Eaton, E. Harris, Williams, Brogden, S. Smith, Hey, Jenkins, Murphy, Satterthwaite, Prosser, Tattersfield, Dyer, Duffy.

Salford v. Hunslet

Date: 16 March 1946
Location: The Willows, Weaste

Challenge Cup third round
Referee: Mr J.E. Taylor (Wakefield)

The Parksiders pulled off one of the most incredible results in both the club's history and in the wider annals of the Challenge Cup when they denied the Red Devils in the quarter-finals of the first post-war competition. Salford, led by the legendary Gus Risman, were bidding for a third consecutive appearance at Wembley and looked assured of a place in the last four when they went into the last three minutes comforted by a three-point lead. Not that such an advantage was necessarily conclusive. A converted try, after all, would put Hunslet in front and there was, in truth, still ample time in which to register such a score. The reality was, though, that Hunslet, with one man short because of a rib injury to centre Cyril Morrell, appeared to all intents and purposes to be dead and gone, as a clearly exhilarated *Yorkshire Post* and *Leeds Mercury* reporter enthused.

'Even Hunslet's long and colourful history contains no finer example of gallant achievement than the victory at Salford,' he wrote. 'Scoring 10 points in the last three minutes with only 12 men, they brought off something as near the impossible as I can remember, and that last crowded five minutes should be a source of pride and inspiration.

'At this point, with the score 8-5 against them, they looked like, and they themselves thought they were, a beaten side. They had tried too far the patience of the gods by presenting Salford with two gift tries, and it seemed as though the gods had retaliated when Morrell had to retire.

'Walkington, one of many weary figures, was inside his own "25" faced by a ring of tacklers. To kick would have given Salford possession, so he passed, and Watson went 30 gallant yards before he was tackled. Walkington was up for the play-the-ball, and from some secret reserve he pulled a burst of speed which took him halfway through the retreating Salford defence.

'Williamson carried on, and as the cover stretched to the wing he turned inside to find White and Thornton running in perfect support. The defence was caught going the wrong way, and it was the hooker's pass that sent Thornton the last 10 yards for a magnificent try.'

Cliff Whitehead's goal put Hunslet in front when it mattered and that clearly knocked the heart out of the Red Devils. Hunslet centre Syd Rookes, who wrapped up the sensational victory, takes up the story. 'Early on, I rambled into Gus Risman, and Syd Williams scored a try from my pass. A bit later I cut through and went down like a stone; half the crowd said I got tripped by Gus Risman – say no more about that, I don't know because I was running away. The referee couldn't send him off, anyway, because he had been selected as captain for the 1946 tour of Australia.

'Later on I intercepted a Risman pass intended for Reg Jones and got the try that sealed our win. I can see Ken Traill now, running at me after I'd scored, with his arms up and the crowd chanting "Rookes for Australia, Rookes for Australia!" It didn't do any good, mind you!'

The fightback not only stunned Salford in what turned out to be Risman's penultimate game for the Red Devils – the great man moving to Workington Town on his return from the Great Britain

---

Salford 8   **Hunslet 15**

Scrum half Billy Thornton, pictured in rampant mood in a match at Headingley, scored the try that helped Hunslet shatter Salford's hopes.

tour. Director Harold Inman had a printers' shop in Hunslet and Rookes remembers: 'On the Monday morning a bloke came in and said, "Eh, Harold, I am sorry!" "What for?" "I had to come away a bit early to miss the crowd and we lost."

'"No, we won," said Harold. "Syd scored a try!"

'Well the other fella went potty, but he was Harold's best customer after that!

'Willie O'Neill was pleased as well. He had been crying when they scored what looked like their winning try, because he'd knocked the ball on. I said to him, "give up will you, we'll win!" But I didn't know.'

Rookes, a powerful presence in the centre, played, according to the *Leeds Mercury*, 'in a fashion that must have made the Tour selectors present search their consciences. (He) was a commanding figure all through, and so was Walkington. Risman, his opposite, was good, but he was outkicked and outgeneralled by the Hunslet captain – an inspiring leader.'

Hunslet also enjoyed significant input from the back three of Whitehead, Des Clarkson and Traill. And Frank Watson – switched to stand-off from his usual scrum half role – also excelled. It all looked like wasted effort, however, as Jones scored for Salford when O'Neill dropped the ball behind his own line, Peter Todd subsequently chasing a kick to add another try despite being outnumbered by Hunslet defenders. But the 22,000 crowd, the highest of the round ahead of 20,475 at Barrow, where Wigan were the visitors, 16,000 at Wakefield (for Workington) and 10,000 for Bramley v. Widnes, were destined to witness a wonderful finish – the early Hunslet absentees excepted. The *Mercury* man concluded: 'Hunslet will never do anything better than this.'

Hunslet: Walkington, Williamson, Morrell, Rookes, O'Neill, Watson, Thornton, Newbound, White, Plenderleith, Whitehead, Clarkson, Traill.

Salford: Risman, Dagnan, Todd, Williams, Edwards, Jones, Harrison, Davies, Day, Gardner, Hartley, Curran, Moses.

HUNSLET v. WAKEFIELD TRINITY

Date: 30 March 1946

Location: Headingley

Challenge Cup semi-final

Referee: Mr G.S. Phillips (Widnes)

In-form Hunslet, after the glory of the quarter-final victory at Salford, slumped to a surprise defeat at the penultimate stage of the Challenge Cup in a match that remains remembered for the wrong reasons. Wakefield reached their first Challenge Cup final for thirty-two years – and their first Wembley outing – after Hunslet winger Willie O'Neill controversially had a try controversially disallowed. The shameful aftermath of that ruling was that a touch judge was hospitalised and a Hunslet supporter arrested as a result of an incident that was the talking point of the 33,000 spectators and has remained so to this day.

The receipts of £4,993 were a record for any code of football in the city up to that time but that fact was the only bright spot for Hunslet, who appeared to have won the game when O'Neill raced the length of the field, beating three defenders on the way. A.L. Drewry of the *Yorkshire Post* and *Leeds Mercury* reported: 'It was a glorious effort, a match-winner if ever there was one, but neither O'Neill nor the Wakefield men had heard the referee whistle for offside as the Hunslet wing gathered Watson's cross kick.

'O'Neill collapsed as he grounded the ball, and so did Teall, his closest pursuer. While they were being revived at one end of the field, ambulance men at the other end were carrying off on a stretcher the touch-judge who had flagged for offside, and two policemen were escorting a spectator from the ground. The touch judge had a broken jaw.'

Although the action of the spectator was inexcusable, his ire was understandable. Frank Watson, who put in the kick that led to O'Neill's run, and centre Syd Rookes were closer than most to the incident that day and both retain vivid memories of the episode many years later. Said Rookes: 'It was a very dubious decision. Frank Watson cross-kicked and the ball rebounded off the Wakefield winger straight into the arms of O'Neill, who was following up. O'Neill then went round that man, up the best stand side and cut across the field. He finished up scoring at the side of the posts and of course everybody would expect that the goal-kicker would kick the goal, which would have put us in front. But George Phillips had blown the whistle. He had never moved from where the scrum had been formed in the first place, and he gave another scrum.' Added Watson: 'That didn't add up. If O'Neill was offside it was a penalty. If the ball had come off the Wakefield man into his arms, it was a try. Having said that, the best referee there's ever been was George Phillips of Widnes – in my view anyhow. But if that try had been allowed Hunslet would have gone to Wembley.

'Jack Pillinger, the lad who assaulted the touch judge, was a big Hunslet supporter who did a lot for the Hunslet club. Unfortunately he got so excited about it all; something like that had never occurred before, and it never did again.'

'No,' said Rookes. 'The thing about Jack Pillinger is that it worked out nice for him in the circumstances. He got three months so he didn't miss any of the next season!'

Hunslet 3   **Wakefield Trinity 7**

HUNSLET *v.* WAKEFIELD TRINITY

Syd Rookes, Ken Traill and Frank Watson apply the type of pressure to the Wakefield defence that led to one of the most controversial incidents in the sport's history.

The unfortunate aspect for the touch judge, Clifford Ramsden, was that he had merely waved his flag to attract the players' attention to the fact that play had been halted. It was also unfortunate that Hunslet's ploy in kicking to O'Neill's wing had not paid off. Coach Jack Walkington had, several weeks earlier, restored Billy Thornton, who had played in the 1934 cup final, to the first team, switching Watson to what had become a problematic stand-off role. And it was from that position that Watson had sparked the controversial incident.

Wakefield captain Billy Stott, who was to earn glory in the final with a last-gasp long-range penalty that scuppered Wigan, put Trinity ahead with a touchline penalty. Hunslet hit back when Thornton went blind at a scrum to send winger Freddie Williamson over, but Wakefield went back in front when winger Denis Baddeley squeezed in at the corner, Stott kicking his second important goal. Hunslet were also hampered by an injury to centre Cyril Morrell, still struggling after the knock to the ribs sustained in the quarter-final win at Salford, who had been targeted in the early stages by Wakefield defenders.

The Parksiders' cause was further hit when Rookes had to depart with cuts to the face but that incident at least led to a sequel that lightened the mood in the Hunslet camp. Rookes tells the tale himself: 'I was carried off and spent all night in hospital. The next night I popped into the Gardener's Arms on Hunslet Moor that night where they were shocked to see me. I said, "what's the matter?" My brother replied that they'd been drinking in my memory. "There been a fella on the radio saying that you'd had 'fatal' injuries". I said "no, 'facial' injuries!"'

Hunslet: Walkington, Williamson, Morrell, Rookes, O'Neill, Watson, Thornton, S. Newbound, White, Plenderleith, Whitehead, Clarkson, Traill.

Wakefield: Teall, Fletcher, Stott, Jones, Baddeley, Rylance, Goodfellow, Wilkinson, Mardon, Higgins, Exley, Howes, Murphy.

Hunslet v. Huddersfield

Date: 20 March 1954

Location: Parkside

Challenge Cup third round

Referee: Mr G.S. Phillips (Widnes)

The holders travelled to Parkside as favourites to emerge victorious in the first meeting in the Challenge Cup between the sides since 1934, when Hunslet had prevailed 12-7 at the semi-final stage.

Fartown had won all four meetings between the teams the previous season, completing the league 'double' and coming out on top in both legs of the Yorkshire Cup meeting. The visitors would, moreover, close the campaign in sixth spot, compared to Hunslet's fifteenth, and they were skippered by Scotsman Dave Valentine who, later in the year, would make history by leading an unfancied Great Britain side to glorious victory in the first World Cup.

Hunslet, too, were plagued by selection problems in the build-up to the game. Welsh full-back Jack Evans was an injury doubt – and would, indeed, prove to be an absentee, Arthur Talbot taking his place – while young prop Colin Cooper and mercurial stand off Brian Gabbitas were on National Service and were unsure of securing release from their duties.

One man, however, who was certain to be available was Alf 'Ginger' Burnell. The scrum half, a central figure in Hunslet's hopes, was under some pressure, having been controversially selected for Great Britain's forthcoming tour of Australasia in a party which was managed and captained by the Parksiders' Hector Rawson and Dickie Williams respectively.

Geoff Gunney was also on the plane for the first Great Britain squad to travel down under by air – and the dynamic forward, with second-row partner Brian Shaw, the rest of the home pack and Burnell, were to prove altogether too much to handle for Huddersfield. Gabbitas – unlike Cooper, able to escape temporarily from the needs of his country – was another key figure as Hunslet accounted for the visitors in imposing fashion before a near-22,000 crowd.

With hooker Stan Smith, bolstered by a driving scrummage, winning the scrums (his 2-1 ascendancy over Harry Bradshaw in the second half was crucial in thwarting Huddersfield's hopes of a comeback) Burnell and Gabbitas treated their supporters to an impressive display of half-back skills. The likes of Valentine, Billy Banks and Ron Rylance, according to Eric Stanger of the *Yorkshire Post*, 'could never seem to guess Burnell's intentions'.

Hunslet's defence was equally imposing against a side forced by its inferiority up front to improvise its attacks, much-vaunted wingers Lionel Cooper and Christian Henderson being starved of any worthwhile possession.

While Hunslet's victory was a triumph of teamwork, Burnell was undoubtedly the glittering jewel in the crown. Making the most of his forwards' dominance, the scrum half scored two tries in the first half – both after breaks direct from the base of the scrum – to put the Parksiders firmly on course for a semi-final berth. And it was Burnell who, in answering his critics in the best possible way, set up the position for winger Fred Williamson to squeeze over in the corner in the second period.

Hunslet 16

Huddersfield 7

HUNSLET v. HUDDERSFIELD

Second-row pair Geoff Gunney and Brian Shaw generated the power that left Huddersfield's bid to retain the Challenge Cup in tatters. The international duo are pictured receiving Yorkshire caps from Hunslet chairman Edgar Meeks.

Two goals by Talbot helped set up a 13-4 lead before Huddersfield threatened to pull the game out of the fire when Valentine 'at last found a gap', racing over thirteen minutes from time for an unconverted try to supplement Pat Devery's two penalties. Hunslet, however, 'were no respecters of reputations' and were in no mood to be diverted; particularly with *We Swept the Seas Before Boys* (a refrain which Burnell admitted caused the hairs on the back of his neck to rise and rendered defeat an impossible concept) ringing in their ears.

Winger Alan Snowden, who would set a club record of 34 tries in 1956/57, rounded off a neat bout of passing and Stanger was moved to ponder: 'Hunslet had swept the holders from the Cup with such a display, in which enterprising back play was harnessed to all-round forward power, that one was left wondering who can put Wembley beyond their reach.' The answer was Halifax.

The Thrum Hallers, coached by former Hunslet 'great' Frank 'Dolly' Dawson, appeared to have done their homework as dreams of an all-Leeds final to match the famous Championship Final of 1938 were shattered in an 18-3 defeat. The Loiners were beaten by Warrington at Swinton, while Hunslet's hopes in an Odsal semi-final watched by 46,961 evaporated when Gabbitas was concussed in the opening minutes, Alfred Drewry of the *Yorkshire Post* reporting: 'Mr George Phillips said quite a lot to Todd, the Halifax centre, but he decided to make more allowance for semi-final nerves than some referees would have done and gave him another chance. The injury to Burnell midway through the first half made a difference to the margin but not, I fancy, to the result. Halifax were eight points ahead when Burnell had to go off.'

Halifax met Warrington at Wembley and drew 4-4 in one of the dourest of finals. Despite that, the replay – at Odsal – attracted a world-record crowd of 102,569. A further 30,000, according to contemporary estimates, broke down the fences to gain entry amid amazing scenes which have entered rugby league folklore. Hunslet, however, were among the outsiders looking in – a recurring theme between 1946 and 1955, when four Challenge Cup semi-finals all ended in defeat.

Hunslet: Talbot, Snowden, Williams, Waite, Williamson, Gabbitas, A. Burnell, Hatfield, Smith, W. Burnell, Shaw, Gunney, Carroll.

Huddersfield: Hunter, Henderson, Rose, Devery, Cooper, Rylance, Banks, Slevin, Bradshaw, Bowden, Large, Briggs, Valentine.

WIGAN v. HUNSLET

Date: 2 May 1959   Championship semi-final
Location: Central Park, Wigan

Hunslet found the key to the Championship final door, twenty-one years after their previous appearance in the victory over Leeds at Elland Road, with a stunning performance that ended Wigan's strong hopes of achieving the cup and league 'double'. The Parksiders, who had made certain of a place in the top four a couple of weeks earlier, had had to wait for the mathematicians to complete their deliberations before knowing which of three Lancashire teams would provide the opposition in the semi-finals. In an era in which league placings were determined by points average (dividing the points scored by those conceded) the final league Saturday of the season would, following consultation with logarithm tables, determine the two semi-finals.

Hunslet had gone into their final game at Mount Pleasant Batley aware that their own result, and those of their rivals, would leave them facing a trip to any of Oldham, St Helens and Wigan. In the event the 35-9 victory, in which former Pontypool winger John Griffiths and loose forward Brian Shaw both scored hat-tricks (centre Billy Walker bagging a brace and winger Ronnie Colin nipping over, and full-back Billy Langton netting four goals) helped ensure, with results elsewhere, that the Parksiders – in third spot – travelled to second-placed Wigan. That, while a tough enough task, was arguably the pairing that Hunslet wanted. Wigan were preparing for a second successive visit to Wembley, where they would defend their grip on the Challenge Cup against Hull, and that little matter may have been on several players' minds when the match, played on Saturday evening because of the counter-attraction of the FA Cup final, kicked off before 23,254 spectators.

Hunslet, with no such diversions, simply overwhelmed the Pie Eaters as they demolished Wigan's 'double' hopes and at the same time gained revenge for the 22-12 Challenge Cup reverse on the same ground, when the gate had been 32,000, a couple of months previously. Adding a touch of extra speed and panache to their trademark wholehearted approach, the Parksiders ruled the roost throughout and had central performers in their back three of Geoff Gunney, Harry Poole and Brian Shaw, who outclassed their opposites Norman Cherrington, Brian McTigue and Roy Evans. Wigan, without skipper Eric Ashton, were turned by the Hunslet assault into a shadow of their usual selves. Scrum half Rees Thomas, the Lance Todd Trophy winner as Man of the Match in the 1958 Challenge Cup final win over Workington Town, struggled throughout against Kevin Doyle. Dennis Tate, drafted in at stand-off in place of Brian Gabbitas, who had a septic leg, controlled Dave Bolton and, if unable to halt the international himself, ensured that he was at least steered into the waiting arms of his forwards.

Tate and Doyle, however, were far more than mere spoilers. Together with Shaw, they were the main tormentors of hapless Wigan who, after having trailed early in the second half, took an underserved lead but found themselves out of contention when Hunslet recorded two tries in a blistering three-minute spell. Both scores resulted from the Parksiders' ability to make the most of

---

Wigan 11   Hunslet 22

Firmly focused, the line-up that steered Hunslet to a first Championship final for twenty-one years.

home errors. Walker was quick to profit from the first slip, sending his centre Alan Preece over, and Gunney was next in the act, slipping a quick pass to Colin who raced away over fifty yards, leaving Great Britain winger Mick Sullivan trailing for a stunning score. The cool Billy Langton added each conversion and Hunslet had booked a meeting with St Helens at Odsal in the final. Colin, who was to finish the season with 34 tries, had opened his account in the first half, when centre Ronnie Stockdill had also touched down. Langton, meanwhile, totalled five goals to continue his record of having played and scored in each of Hunslet's games during the season. The feat had only been achieved once before, by Widnes' Jimmy Hoey in 1932/33.

Wigan, unarguably second best, were left with dreams of the 'double' in tatters and with extra injury worries ahead of the Challenge Cup final against Hull. Sullivan, who needed stitches in his knee, was a major doubt and there were also concerns over South African goal kicker Fred Griffiths. Both, however, were able to feature, together with Ashton, as the Pie Eaters crushed the Airlie Birds 30-13, a record score for a Challenge Cup final and a result that added extra lustre to an achievement at Central Park that came as no surprise to close observers of matters at Parkside.

Hunslet had reached the top-four play-offs with a series of strong performances that had garnered 27 victories and 3 draws in their 38 league games. The season had opened relatively indifferently with a defeat at, ironically, Wigan, followed by draws with Hull and, in the Yorkshire Cup, at Wakefield Trinity, which were interspersed with a 10-7 victory at Post Office Road against Featherstone Rovers.

Above: Geoff Gunney crashes over for a try against Wigan at Parkside. Brian Shaw, another of the famous back three of Poole, Gunney and Shaw, monitors events.

Right: Billy Langton, a fine full-back, played and scored in each of Hunslet's matches in 1958/59 to emulate the record set by Widnes's Jimmy Hoey twenty-six years earlier. Langton went on to earn a well-deserved benefit in 1964/65.

Opposite page: Hunslet missed out to Wigan in the chase for Billy Boston's services in the early 1950s. The great Welshman, generally kept under wraps when he faced the Parksiders, managed to cross the whitewash in the 1959 Championship semi-final. The last laugh, though, was with Hunslet on this occasion.

Hunslet lost the replay with Trinity 15-11 at Parkside, before a 16,835 crowd, but that exit presaged a three-match winning run in the league that culminated in a 13-5 victory over Huddersfield in which Walker, who switched between the wing and centre throughout the season, got off the mark with two tries. Walker was to come agonisingly close to beating Alan Snowden's record, set two years earlier, of 34 tries in a season, finishing just one short at the close of the campaign with no return from his appearances in the championship semi-final or the final itself. The flyer went on to score in the next four games, including the 31-15 reverse at St Helens before a 15,000 crowd at

Knowsley Road, while full-back Billy Langton was continuing to register at least one goal in every match in a sequence that would lead to him entering the code's record books.

Two days after that defeat against the Saints, Hunslet staged their home game against Leeds on unusual territory. The Parksiders opted to switch the venue to Elland Road, reviving memories of the 1938 Championship final, and were rewarded with a 15-8 victory, but a disappointing attendance of 19,289.

Wins over Featherstone Rovers, Bradford Northern, Batley, Castleford and Wigan followed in the upwards surge, the 29-21 verdict over the Pie Eaters before 12,000 at Parkside proving to be a real high-scoring thriller in an era of generally low scores. Hunslet went down the following week, 19-12 at Derwent Park, Workington, but only five more league games would be lost – at the testing arenas of Wakefield, Hull KR, Halifax, Huddersfield and Oldham.

Perhaps the highlight of the 17 subsequent league wins was the 19-11 victory over St Helens at Parkside in late January, when 13,500 thrilled to a performance in which the Parksiders led 10-3 at half-time and prevailed with tries for Colin Byrom, Shaw and Gabbitas, with Langton (3), Doyle and Poole adding goals. Sadly, Hunslet would be unable to deny the Saints in the Championship final.

Wigan: Cunliffe, Boston, Griffiths, Holden, Sullivan, Bolton, Thomas, Bretherton, Sayer, Collier, Cherrington, McTigue, Evans.

Hunslet: Langton, Colin, Stockdill, Preece, Walker, Tate, Doyle, Hatfield, Smith, Eyre, Poole, Gunney, Shaw.

HUNSLET *v.* ST HELENS

Date: 16 May 1959   **Championship final**
Location: Odsal Stadium, Bradford   **Referee:** Mr G. Wilson (Dewsbury)

The epic Championship final of 1959, rated by many as arguably the best of the genre, is remembered primarily for the performance of one man. Unfortunately for Hunslet, that player was wearing the red and white of St Helens rather than the myrtle, white and flame of a club that had also been in the running for his services several years earlier.

The player in question was South African winger Tom van Vollenhoven, who entered the annals of rugby league folklore with a length-of-the-field try that swung the pendulum towards the Lancashire side in the immortal Jim Sullivan's last game as coach. Hunslet, after having established an early 12-4 lead, appeared to be in control and, having beaten the Saints 19-11 at Parkside four months earlier in a league fixture, had no real cause for concern. There was little obvious danger when Vollenhoven was given possession close to his own line, with twenty-four minutes gone. Facing him was Billy Walker, one of the best defenders around and a man, moreover, who was under strict instructions to monitor the South African flyer closely throughout. On this one occasion, however, Walker found himself sucked in by centre Duggie Greenall, and the 'Voll' made the most of his slim opportunity. With little space to play with, and hemmed in on the touchline by a committed posse of Parksiders, Vollenhoven produced his first minor miracle, accelerating past the initial line of defence with a remarkable and blistering change of pace. With three defenders already sprawling, another was led astray by virtue of a startling sidestep. Four Hunslet players having been disposed of, yet two more would-be tacklers were duly denied by the South African's trademark hand off. Even Hunslet fans – some, admittedly, grudgingly – were moved to applaud as Tom van Vollenhoven touched down. His score, however, was no consolation effort. Instead, it galvanised the Saints, who had finished top of the table to Hunslet's third, to a match-winning performance in which the winger completed a hat-trick and a sensational twenty-minute spell, perhaps as impressive as any seen by a club side, in which twenty-eight points were scored without reply to put the issue beyond doubt within three minutes of the second half getting under way. The *Yorkshire Post*, recognising the fact that the 52,560 crowd had witnessed something truly special, eulogised: 'Hunslet were willing, resolute – and outclassed. There was just nothing they could do against the speed of St Helens' passing and the lightning thrusts of Alex Murphy in the middle and van Vollenhoven on the right flank. St Helens in this period played football of a standard one sees perhaps two or three times in a lifetime.

'Remember, this was no piling-on-the-agony frolic against dispirited opposition. When van Vollenhoven put the match to the fuse St Helens were eight points down. Hunslet contested every point with the utmost determination but when it came to the pinch they were wanting for speed.'

The Parksiders, however, played a full role in an epic that delighted the 52,560 crowd. Hunslet had taken the game to St Helens with Ronnie Stockdill and Kevin Doyle crossing for early tries, full-back Billy Langton adding three goals. Stand-off Brian Gabbitas was rated as Hunslet's best

Hunslet 22   **St Helens 44**

It is doubtful whether St Helens would have beaten Hunslet in the 1959 Championship final without the presence of Tom van Vollenhoven. There was no way through this time, however, for the explosive South African.

performer, with Doyle also earning plaudits. 'Preece,' wrote the *Yorkshire Post* reporter 'gave the best display I have ever seen from him at centre, and Poole was the best member of a pack made to look less light than usual by St Helens' superior speed.'

St Helens, who had totalled an incredible 1,005 points in their 38 league games – surpassing Huddersfield's record of 996 in 1911/12 – duly lifted the championship for the first time in six years, Smith, Alex Murphy and Dick Huddart also crossing the whitewash in support of van Vollenhoven. The Parksiders' response, though, was impressive. Back-row men Geoff Gunney and Harry Poole forced their way over, Langton adding each conversion, but it wasn't enough to deny their opponents in what remains possibly St Helens' finest performance.

Hunslet, however, would surely have been crowned champions but for the presence of van Vollenhoven. The *Yorkshire Post* wrote of his first try: 'Throughout a run of 70 yards he was forced by the inside cover to stay within a yard of the touchline. Yet he managed to beat Preece, Langton and Shaw on the *outside* to finish near enough to the posts for Rhodes to land the goal. No wonder they chaired him off the field. A really great winger, this South African.'

Not bad for a player who, suffering from chest problems as a child and regarded as fragile, hadn't even touched an oval ball in the rugby-mad South Africa until the age of eleven. And the dividing line between glory and near-misses in sport is exemplified by the fact that Vollenhoven had been a doubt right up to the kick-off, turning out with his left thigh heavily strapped but fighting off the effects of the injury until after scoring the second of his three tries.

Hunslet: Langton, Colin, Stockdill, Preece, Walker, Gabbitas, Doyle, Hatfield, Smith, Eyre, Poole, Gunney, Shaw.

St Helens: Rhodes, Vollenhoven, Greenall, McGinn, Prinsloo, Smith, Murphy, Terry, McKinney, Prescott, Briggs, Huddart, Karalius.

HUNSLET v. HULL KINGSTON ROVERS

Date: 27 October 1962   **Yorkshire Cup final**
Location: Headingley   **Referee:** Mr R. Gelder (Wilmslow)

Hunslet upset the form book to win the Yorkshire Cup for the first time since 1907 – when the trophy had been the first of the 'All Four Cups' collection to be gathered – and deny Rovers the chance to retrieve a piece of silver that had not rested at Craven Park since the victory over the Parksiders in 1929. Most pundits believed that the result was little more than a forgone conclusion. The Rugby Football League had, in 1962/63, introduced a three-year experiment with two divisions (to be abandoned after a couple of years because of dwindling attendances) and Hunslet had been unable to qualify for the top flight. Hull KR, by contrast, had come eighth in the thirty-team table the previous season, and would finish a reasonably respectable twelfth at the close of the campaign. Well led by former Hunslet favourite Harry Poole, the Robins were about to enjoy a period of unprecedented success on the East Coast, and there were few who anticipated anything other than a Hull KR victory. The list included Leslie Temlett of the *Yorkshire Evening Post* but the journalist cautioned: 'I do not share any belief that the result is a foregone conclusion.

'Hunslet's blend of youth and experience make them a formidable combination. Men like Fred Ward, their coach and loose forward, Jeff Stevenson and Brian Gabbitas are all capable of match-winning inspiration – or scores.'

Temlett was precipitant and perceptive. The Parksiders, after a couple of dismal seasons since having reached the Championship final in 1959, were regrouping under Ward, who had been snapped up from York after previous spells with Leeds and Keighley, and the side was to gain promotion at the close of the season as Division Two champions. Hunslet had, moreover, claimed the scalps of three Division One teams en route to the final. A Wakefield Trinity side that had only been denied its own 'All Four Cups' feat the previous season through losing 14-5 to Huddersfield in the Championship final, had been swamped 34-9 at Parkside in the first round. Hull, next to travel to south Leeds, were accounted for 18-7, and Halifax were edged 7-6 at Thrum Hall at the penultimate stage. The Parksiders, therefore, had no reason to fear any opposition and, despite one or two injury scares in the build-up, the match progressed in a manner that suggested that fate was, perhaps, on their side. Great Britain second-row forward Geoff Gunney, a doubt because of cold in his gums, was unable to play and his place was taken by Cliff Lambert. The pragmatic Arthur Render was selected on the left wing while former international Stevenson, who had been bracketed with young Ronnie Watts for the scrum half berth during the week, was given the nod. Poole, meanwhile, passed a fitness test for the Robins; a state of affairs that he would perhaps come to regret.

Hunslet played well, as should have been expected given the status of their victims in previous rounds, while Hull KR suffered a series of mishaps that caused Temlett to reflect: 'They could scarcely have had worse luck if they had broken every looking glass in their homes, walked under a

Hunslet 12   Hull KR 2

Fred Ward displays the Yorkshire Cup to the crowd. Forty-four years later, he remains the last Hunslet captain to collect a major trophy.

succession of ladders between home and rendezvous, and spent the journey from Hull to Headingley taking pot shots at robins.

'To lose the toss was bad enough with a strong wind blowing from end to end, but that was a minor misfortune compared with the disasters to follow.'

Hunslet could respond with the eternal truism in sport that successful teams make their own luck, and that was the case when the Parksiders took an early lead in only the second minute. Full-back Billy Langton, attempting an early penalty, was unfortunate when his shot hit the outside of a post. Second row Billy Baldwinson, however, followed up at pace and judged the flight of the spinning ball better than Rovers full-back Cyril Kellett, pouncing for a superb opportunist try that Langton improved for an early five-point lead. Hull KR never recovered. Indeed, matters deteriorated badly.

Poole was stretchered off on the half hour and, five minutes after the interval, the Robins were dealt another shattering blow when centre Mike Blackmore had to withdraw with a broken shoulder. Stand-off Dave Elliott spent most of the game concussed and Kingston Rovers finished with only ten players, scrum half Hatch retiring in the closing stages, by which time the issue had been resolved, with a leg injury. 'We were down to eleven men including me when Mike Blackmore went off,' says Elliott. 'It was even worse really, we already had Johnny Moore sitting in the stand with a broken leg.

HUNSLET v. HULL KINGSTON ROVERS

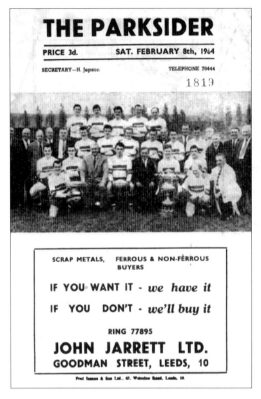

THE PARKSIDER

PRICE 3d. SAT. FEBRUARY 8th, 1964

SECRETARY—H. Jepson TELEPHONE 78444

1819

SCRAP METALS, FERROUS & NON-FERROUS
BUYERS

IF YOU WANT IT - *we have it*

IF YOU DON'T - *we'll buy it*

RING 77895

JOHN JARRETT LTD.

GOODMAN STREET, LEEDS, 10

Fred Inman & Son Ltd., 63, Waterloo Road, Leeds, 10.

Hunslet added the Division Two championship to the Yorkshire Cup in 1962/63. The following season's programme cover celebrated the double achievement.

'Hunslet were lucky, their first try was fortunate after the ball bounced out off an upright and they were playing in their home city. But they were a very good side packed with talented players.'

Hunslet drew some criticism for not making more use of their numerical advantage but Ward, as shrewd a coach as any around, could point to the result as evidence that there was no pressing need. The Parksiders' victory was founded on solid defence, with Hull KR rarely looking capable of scoring while boasting a full complement, and Hunslet had in Stevenson a schemer of high intelligence who ensured that his side were always fully in control. With the Robins, caught in a stranglehold, limited to a penalty in the second half by Kellett, Hunslet had to do no more than tighten their grip with a spectacular solo try by powerful centre Geoff Shelton, which Langton improved. And there was delight for the Hunslet supporters in the 22,742 crowd when prop Dennis Hartley, a capture from Doncaster who would go on to terrorise Australia in the 1970 Ashes Series success Down Under, dropped a goal that, many years later, remains vivid in coach Fred Ward's mind. 'We had been on their line for about five minutes and we weren't getting anywhere, so I told Stevie to go for a drop goal. Anyhow, somehow or other the ball ended up with Dennis who must have automatically thought "drop a goal". And he did. I think it was the only time he kicked the ball in his entire career.

'It's funny how these things work out. We lost Geoff Gunney before the game because of illness. You could count the number of matches Geoff missed on one hand and still have enough fingers left for a V-sign, so that was a blow. But that brought Billy Baldwinson in, which wasn't bad for me because he liked to come short.'

Left: Second row Billy Baldwinson's opportunist try sent Hunslet on the way to a notable victory. The loyal packman is pictured with club officials at a presentation.

Right: Stand-off Brian Gabbitas was at the core of the Hunslet side for over a decade. Having quit the game after sustaining a broken jaw in an incident at Huddersfield, 'Gabby' switched to amateur soccer in his retirement.

John Bapty of the *Yorkshire Evening Post* reflected: 'The Yorkshire Cup is on show at Parkside for the first time for more than half a century and Hunslet folk, rightly, are taking pride in displaying it.

'They regard it as a sign that better times are on the way and, of course, they are entitled to do that for they have taken this trophy as a Second Division club that has beaten four First Division clubs.

'But at the same time they have a full recognition of the fact that... Kingston Rovers finished with 10 men, although by the time the limping Hatch had gone to the dressing room the Cup was safely in Hunslet's hands.

'Kingston Rovers' Tyson and his four forwards and the gallant backs had played themselves into the ground, but their work in the first half when they were so resolute against the wind, and their football with 11 men in the second half gave them a place of their own in the history of the competition.

'But Stevenson (worth his weight in gold for Hunslet in this game), Ward, Gabbitas, Lambert and the others in Parkside colours will say that they snatched five points and a lead they never lost when Hull Kingston were at strength. And they, too, are entitled to argue that things might have been different had they been able to field their full-strength side. They had to look around for wing three-quarters.'

Ward, the last Hunslet captain to lift a major trophy, recalls how he almost missed out on the moment. 'I wanted Jeff Stevenson to go up for the Cup. But Jeff said, "no Fred, you're the captain, you go." And I can't remember the rest. Perhaps I was too excited.'

Hunslet: Langton, Lee, Shelton, Preece, Render, Gabbitas, Stevenson, Hartley, Prior, Eyre, Baldwinson, Lambert, Ward.

Hull KR: Kellett, Paul, Major, Blackmore, Harris, Elliott, Hatch, Grice, Lockwood, J. Drake, Tyson, Taylor, Poole.

WAKEFIELD TRINITY v. HUNSLET

Date: 12 February 1964
Location: Belle Vue, Wakefield

Challenge Cup first round replay
Referee: Mr T.W. Watkinson (Manchester)

The 1963/64 Challenge Cup will long be remembered as the year of the draw. Eventual winners Widnes certainly achieved their success the hard way. The usual five-match sequence for the sides fortunate enough to reach Wembley was extended, in the Chemics' case, to an amazing ten games while runners-up Hull KR played eight matches.

Hull KR's similarly tortuous route to the Twin Towers culminated in the most dramatic of semi-final ties with Division Two leaders Oldham, who had stunned the sporting world with a 7-5 quarter-final win at Hunslet despite having lost their captain in the early stages with a leg injury. The teams drew the initial pairing 5-5 and the Roughyeds – a huge power in the Challenge Cup prior to the Wembley era – looked on course for a first final since 1927 when they led 17-14 in extra time in the first replay at Headingley. Failing light, however, caused the referee to draw a halt to the game. The RFL ruled another replay, which Hull won 12-2, leaving Oldham perhaps regretting their win at Parkside, where the competition had opened with the eagerly anticipated visit of Wakefield Trinity. Trinity had won the Cup in each of the previous two seasons but were far from feared in south Leeds, having lost 12-7 at Parkside in late January.

That first round tie, in common with the 1964 competition as a whole genre, ended in a draw, Billy Langton kicking two goals to counter Neil Fox's brace of penalties, and all was set for a midweek afternoon replay at Belle Vue. Hunslet official Harry Jepson, a schoolteacher, ensured that he would see at least the second half when, counting the takings after the Parkside clash, he looked outside and noted that it was not yet dark. Negotiations were successfully completed for a later kick-off than had been initially envisaged in an era in which no club boasted floodlights, and the clubs were rewarded with an attendance of 20,822 that, added to 19,937 at Hunslet, meant that a total of 40,759 witnessed the epic tie.

All had to be impressed by the Parksiders' pack, in which player-coach Fred Ward (a player who had bucked the usual trend by moving backwards from the prop position through his career rather than in the opposite direction) excelled at loose forward. Second row Geoff Gunney, head shaven to help gain those vital extra inches in his headlong charges at the opposition, was another massive presence, and props Ken Eyre and Dennis Hartley ran riot. The backs duly prospered. Ronnie Watts, deputising at scrum half for the injured Jeff Stevenson, sparked his backline to fine effect. Stand-off Brian Gabbitas was at his mercurial best and the straight-running Geoff Shelton was reaching the form that would gain him international recognition and the status of being arguably the best centre in the game. The *Yorkshire Evening Post* was moved to reflect that, but for the Herculean efforts of Trinity's Don Metcalfe at full-back and Colin Greenwood on the wing, Hunslet would have doubled their score. Even so, Wakefield had the best of starts when Neil Fox kicked an early penalty. Hunslet, however, were unfazed and, with their forwards taking a grip, forced their way back into contention.

Wakefield Trinity 7   Hunslet 14

Hunslet 1963/64. The Division Two champions and Yorkshire Cup holders are pictured prior to entertaining reigning Division One champions Swinton on the opening day of the season. From left to right, back row: Geoff Gunney, John Griffiths, Bill Ramsey, Ken Eyre, D. Smith, Fred Ward, Denis Hartley. Front row: Bernard Prior, Geoff Shelton, Jeff Stevenson, Alan Preece, Billy Langton, Brian Gabbitas.

Gabbitas and Shelton, irrepressible, carved open the home defence with an incisive attack, and Gunney was on hand to crash over underneath the posts for Langton to convert.

Langton, crucially, went on to kick four goals, while the Parksiders scored the try of the game (and, possibly, of the season) when powerful Welsh winger John Griffiths raced over from a pass by Shelton that the *Evening Post*'s reporter described as 'one of the greatest passes I have seen by a player as he went down in a two-man tackle'. He added: 'In fairness to Trinity, it must be said that five of Hunslet's points came when Metcalfe, who had a head injury and concussion, was off the field. Also that loose forward Haigh was dazed early on. But I don't think it made much difference.'

John Allen, of the *Wakefield Express*, was also impressed. He wrote: 'Unfortunately, like the forwards, the Belle Vue backs were just not good enough to bear more than slight comparison with sparkling Hunslet, the cute visitors often switching the direction of assaults with a nonchalance that put the seal of greatness on their crisp movements.'

Ward's men went on to dispose of Batley 14-6 at Mount Pleasant, before 11,500 folk, in the second round. But, now among the favourites to win the competition, Hunslet's dreams were shattered by the quarter-final defeat at the hands of depleted Oldham at a rain-swept Parkside.

Wakefield: Metcalfe, Greenwood, Rushton, Fox, Coetzer, Poynton, Holliday, Wilkinson, Oakes, M. Sampson, Briggs, Turner, Haigh.

Hunslet: Langton, Griffiths, Shelton, Preece, Thompson, Gabbitas, Watts, Hartley, Prior, Eyre, Baldwinson, Gunney, Ward.

Hunslet v. Oldham

Date: 6 February 1965
Location: Parkside

Challenge Cup first round
Referee: Mr E. Leach (St Helens)

The general perception of Hunslet's glorious Challenge Cup exploits of 1965 is that, the final against Wigan apart, the Parksiders' toughest tests were in the semi-final against Wakefield Trinity and, to a degree, at the quarter-final stage against Leeds. While both were notable wins, it could be argued that Hunslet's finest performance during the cup run was in the first round.

Few gave the Parksiders' any hope of progress when the draw, made live on BBC TV, paired them with Oldham. Home advantage was useful, and Hunslet were going into the competition in the higher echelons of the league, having spent much of the first half of the season tucked into third place behind St Helens and Wigan. But Fred Ward's charges, who had been boosted by the arrival in September of scrum half Alan Marchant in a £3,500 transfer from Halifax, had started to slip a little. Between the end of November and the close of January Hunslet had lost five of their eight games, and two of those defeats had been at the hands of the Roughyeds.

Oldham had travelled to south Leeds in early December and returned home across the Pennines with a 7-4 verdict in which Hunslet had been limited to two Arthur Render goals. And the New Year started badly for the Parksiders with a trip to the Watersheddings in which Eddie Waring and his TV viewers were treated to a 36-7 stroll by the Lancastrians. The author's mother commented 'and pigs can fly' to the then-twelve-year-old's view that Hunslet would win easily, and there was little justification in attempting to pursue an argument. Our porky brethren, however, were regularly seen hurtling across the skies for many years afterwards as the Parksiders belied previously indifferent form and the absence of important figures to record a fully merited win. Oldham also lacked key men, with player/coach Frank Dyson a notable absentee. Hunslet, however, were without injured no six Brian Gabbitas and prop Dennis Hartley, who was suspended. Fred Ward opted to move Alan Preece from the centre to stand-off, with Arthur Render taking Preece's spot. The coach also switched Ken Eyre to open-side prop and drafted in Billy Baldwinson in the blind-side berth. Baldwinson went on to produce a superb performance, running Eyre – a heavyweight prop forward with a remarkable change of pace and an astonishing sidestep – close for the Man of the Match as Hunslet mastered the redoubtable Oldham pack.

The *Oldham Evening Chronicle's* Roger Halstead reflected: 'Alf Mumberson and Ken Wilson were given a prize lesson by Baldwinson and Eyre, two props playing out of position, whose strong running did much to make Oldham's forwards look a weary, lead footed lot.

'Eyre was always foraging, breaking tackles and letting the ball go. He scored the first try after smartly picking up a long ball, and laid on the second with a strong burst before handing on to Render, who had all the time in the world to put winger Barry Lee in at the corner.

'Baldwinson wasn't far behind his front row colleague, and while the pair cashed in on the craft of second row Geoff Gunney and loose forward Fred Ward, Oldham hadn't a man to distribute effectively.'

Hunslet 12   Oldham 4

Hunslet v. Oldham

Hunslet chairman Harold Inman worked a flanker on the authorities by rearranging an 'A' team game for the morning of the Challenge Cup tie with Oldham as a means of wiping out a suspension on scrum half Alan Marchant. Inman went on to preside over the sale of Parkside in 1973.

Oldham captain Dave Parker and his set played into Hunslet's hands by regularly turning the ball inside, with second row Peter Smethurst a prime culprit, and the Roughyeds' mercurial scrum half Jackie Pycroft was kept under wraps by Marchant. The visitors, with few opportunities, proved to be profligate when stand-in winger Joe Collins fluffed two rare opportunities, spilling a kick when given a clear chance and being unable to take a difficult pass from stand-off Stan McLeod. McLeod had been the Roughyeds' only real threat, a thirty-yard run testing Hunslet who otherwise were in control defensively throughout, limiting the visitors to two goals by full-back Geoff Sims, who missed with five other attempts, including one fairly simple effort. Hunslet, after falling behind to an early Sims penalty, quickly corrected matters when Eyre was on hand to finish off a raid by centre Geoff Shelton, crashing over At Mother Benson's End to give the Parksiders a lead they were never to lose. Full-back Billy Langton added the extras and, as half-time approached, a penalty to put Hunslet in control.

Oldham threatened when Simms kicked a goal but Eyre, again, was an inspiration, dousing the visitors' joy with the charge that led to Lee's touchdown. Ward, with the Roughyeds devoid of imagination and Preece withdrawn through injury – Ray Abbey taking his place – was content to sit on the match-winning lead for the remainder of the game. And there was certainly no way back for the visitors when Langton landed a penalty two minutes from time after Marchant had been obstructed. Revenge had been gained for the shock quarter-final reverse of the previous season, and something other than pigs was stirring in the air. Hunslet did not, at that stage, know it; but they were on their way to Wembley!

Hunslet: Langton, Griffiths, Shelton, Render, Lee, Preece, Marchant, Eyre, Prior, Baldwinson, Ramsey, Gunney, Ward. Sub: Abbey.

Oldham: Sims, Collins, Donovan, McCormack, Elliott, McLeod, Pycroft, Mumberson, McIntyre, Wilson, Bott, Smethurst, Parker.

HUNSLET *v.* LEEDS

Date: 13 March 1965
Location: Parkside

Challenge Cup third round
Referee: Mr R.L. Thomas (Oldham)

Hunslet, generally recognised as marginally the best side in the city during the 1964/65 season, had revenge on their minds as the quarter-final tie against their old rivals approached. The teams had yet to meet in the league (home advantage would prove to be crucial in the fixtures played over the Easter weekend) but the Loiners had won the pre-season Lazenby Cup fixture at Parkside 18-2 and had then walloped Hunslet 25-8 in the Yorkshire Cup first round tie at Headingley, easing clear after having led just 5-2 at half-time.

Within twenty-four hours Hunslet had snared Alan Marchant from Halifax. His impact was immediate as the Parksiders, who had lost two of their opening four league games, went on to win their next seven fixtures to head to the heights of the table. The arrival of the Challenge Cup, and victories over Oldham and Batley, had diverted attention from the domestic programme. Hunslet, in fact, had lost all their league games since the first round success against Oldham, sustaining defeats at the hands of Featherstone Rovers, Wakefield Trinity and Hull, but the focus was clearly on reaching Wembley and supporters were confident of victory when the Loiners arrived at Parkside.

Hunslet's prospects were helped by the fact that Leeds were without goal-kicking full-back Robin Dewhurst, but coach Fred Ward had his own problems, with prop Ken Eyre – the match-winner in the first round against Oldham – and second row Bill Ramsey notable absentees. Ward, who opted for Billy Baldwinson in the front row, switched himself from loose forward to the second row and gave Colin Taylor the number fourteen shirt (few loose forwards, in that era, were prepared to risk wearing the 'unlucky' thirteen).

A crowd of 13,000 – significantly lower than had been anticipated, with few admissions in the twenty minutes before kick-off in a reversal of the 'norm' for rugby league games – witnessed a real thriller in which Hunslet were grateful for a late miss by young Loiner Trevor Oldroyd who, offered a penalty attempt from a relatively comfortable position, was unable to garner the points that could have forced a replay. Oldroyd, who moved to Batley shortly afterwards, had also been wide with an earlier effort but, while there were several pundits who reckoned that a draw would have been a fair result, few, if any, believed that Hunslet deserved to lose.

The Parksiders' pack, despite the absence of Eyre and Ramsey, was generally on top as Baldwinson again confirmed his undoubted qualities, and the early ascendancy helped Hunslet to a seven-point lead that, in the event, proved to be unassailable. Bernard Prior, recognised as one of the best ball-securing hookers in the game, had arrived at Hunslet four years earlier, together with £10,000 and Norman Burton, as part of the £13,500 deal that saw loose forward Brian Shaw head to Headingley. The Parksiders, over time, got much the better of that arrangement. Prior was rarely beaten in the scrum count and, on this occasion, ensured a huge amount of possession for his side that proved to be the seminal factor.

Hunslet 7   Leeds 5

Matches between Hunslet and Leeds were tense affairs, as the expressions on the faces of Alan Marchant, Arthur Render and Bernard Prior in a league clash played less than a month after the Challenge Cup victory clearly illustrate.

The *Yorkshire Evening Post's* John Bapty wrote: 'Hunslet moved onto the ball but – and this is something they must think about – they were unable with overwhelming scrummage advantage to produce another try against men who tackled as well as a Leeds side has tackled, and who revealed in long breaks from their own 25 attacking possibilities which suggested that things could have been different had they had a fair share of the ball.'

The Hunslet six, with Marchant's impact at scrum half, ensured that they didn't and, with points at a premium, the sides were limited to a single try each. Welsh winger John Griffiths powered over for Hunslet's, with full-back Billy Langton kicking two goals for that vital seven-point lead. Leeds went on to have the better of the second half and grabbed their touchdown when Scottish winger Ron Cowan raced over. Oldroyd, however, could only kick one goal but the *Evening Post's* WHO was happy for Geoff Gunney, reflecting: 'It was a game in which all tried and among the memories will be one of Gunney slashing in as though he had the key to Wembley's gates in his hands.' He also gave credit to Leeds' Scottish centre Drew Broatch, who would later play for and coach New Hunslet: 'He has stepped in a month or two from the ordinary ranks to high class and thinking of him and (his co-centre) Dick Gemmell, and of Marchant, Brian Gabbitas and Geoff Shelton, one wonders just what they would do in the game if Rugby League provided the room it once did for the backs.'

Hunslet, however, were not too concerned about the style of the match. They were in the semi-finals of the Challenge Cup for the first time for ten years and, after four successive defeats at the penultimate stage, had unfinished business on the agenda.

Hunslet: Langton, Griffiths, Shelton, Preece, Lee, Gabbitas, Marchant, Hartley, Prior, Baldwinson, Ward, Gunney, Taylor.

Leeds: Simpson, Cowan, Broach, Gemmell, Wriglesworth, Oldroyd, Batten, Clark, Lockwood, Walker, Morgan, Neumann, Chamberlain. Subs: Ratcliffe, Sykes.

Hunslet v. Wakefield Trinity

Date: 10 April 1965

Location: Headingley, Leeds

Challenge Cup semi-final

Referee: Mr D.T.H. Davies (Manchester)

The Challenge Cup setbacks of 1946, 1948, 1954 and 1955 were, if not forgotten, at least assuaged by a victory based on superb defence, pragmatic tactics and a slice of good fortune in the all-important first try of the game. That came twelve minutes from time, when centre Alan Preece crossed for one of the most important touchdowns in the club's history. The score, although unconverted by full-back Billy Langton, broke Wakefield's hearts. With time running out, burly Welsh winger John Griffiths crashed over in the corner. And a famous win was sealed when Langton landed a long-range penalty in the closing stages.

Hunslet were at strength, while Trinity lacked scrum half Ray Owen, who was replaced by a more than capable deputy in Terry Hopwood. Wakefield, who had appeared in the 1960, 1962 and 1963 Challenge Cup finals, were red-hot favourites, although it was difficult to see why. Trinity, it was true, went into the game on the back of a winning run stretching back to the previous December. But the last side to beat them had, in fact, been Hunslet, with a resounding 20-6 success at Belle Vue. And Wakefield had hardly been inspiring in the 4-0 quarter-final victory, also at Belle Vue, against a Blackpool Borough outfit that would finish bottom of the table but that had confirmed that a policy of harassing an admittedly classy bunch of players could pay dividends.

Hunslet, for their part, knew all about how to beat Wakefield and had, in fact, held the upper hand in meetings between the sides for a number of years. Quite apart from that league success four months earlier, the Parksiders had dumped Wakefield – then the holders, in two consecutive seasons – out of the competition in 1964, while Trinity had been hammered 34-9 in the first round on the Parksiders' way to winning the Yorkshire Cup in 1962.

The upper hand again rested with Hunslet who, with a sensible display of safety-first football, outwitted Wakefield on a dry pitch which had been expected to favour Trinity's speedy backs. Their approach wasn't universally popular but Challenge Cup semi-finals are the last arena in which style counts for anything. Victory, within the rules, is all-important and Alfred Drewry of the *Yorkshire Post* summed up: 'Hunslet's football had all the characteristics of the place where it was nurtured – no airs and graces, no flights of fancy; it was down-to-earth, straightforward stuff, first, last and all the time. Wembley was the objective, and if it had to be reached at the expense of entertainment for outsiders, too bad for the outsiders.' He added: 'Most people blamed Hunslet for the humdrum quality of the match because they had infinitely more possession. Casual spectators will be surprised to learn that Prior's share of the ball from the scrums was no more than 60 per cent. Hunslet seemed to have 80 per cent of the play because they retained possession more efficiently than the more adventurous (and more panicky) Wakefield side.

'Hunslet's domination can be judged by a recital of what happened after the first try, scored with 12 minutes to go. Hunslet got possession from the kick-off and retained it for 33 play-the-ball

---

Hunslet 8   Wakefield Trinity 0

HUNSLET *v.* WAKEFIELD TRINITY

Centre Alan Preece and second row Geoff Gunney defend in spectacular style. Prolific Wakefield rarely looked like scoring against the committed Parksiders.

operations, interrupted only by a penalty from which Langton found touch and Hunslet heeled, and ended only when they scored the second time.

'Ironically, after so much scheming, Hunslet's first try was the result of a Hunslet mistake. When Ward's pass went astray, the ball bounced eccentrically into the path of Preece, who snatched it eagerly to run past an off-balance defence.'

Drewry added the highest possible praise, stating: 'I reckon that the forwards who more than 60 years ago became known as the "Terrible Six" would have had full marks for Ramsey, Prior, Gunney, Eyre, Ward and Hartley.

'And I reckon, too, that the legendary Albert Goldthorpe would have had full marks for Marchant, Gabbitas and the others in the Hunslet backs had he been there to listen to the old war song when Preece had gone in for the try that settled the argument.'

For Geoff Gunney, the only survivor from the 1955 semi-final defeat by Barrow, the win capped a fine season in which he had been recalled to the Great Britain side after an eight-year gap. It also eased the long-term pain of former player-coach Jack Walkington, who reflected: 'Today made up for the biggest disappointment of my career.

'I know just how Wakefield feel. We were just as warm favourites to beat them on this ground in the 1946 semi-final as they were to beat Hunslet today. Nothing went right for us that day. This time it was Wakefield's turn on the rack.'

Hunslet came in for strong criticism from many quarters for their safety-first approach. But another local team with a certain reputation were delighted. Leeds United, who had already qualified for the FA Cup final, sent two congratulatory telegrams before Ward and his men had left the dressing rooms – one from the 'Leeds United Dressing Room', the other to Hunslet chairman Harold Inman from his United counterpart Harry Reynolds.

Hunslet: Langton, Griffiths, Shelton, Preece, Lee, Gabbitas, Marchant, Hartley, Prior, Eyre, Ramsey, Gunney, Ward.

Wakefield: Metcalfe, Jones, Thomas, Fox, Coetzer, Poynton, Hopwood, Vines, Shepherd, Campbell, Sampson, Haigh, Holliday.

HUNSLET v. WIGAN

Date: 8 May 1965
Location: Wembley

Challenge Cup final
Referee: Mr J. Manley (Warrington)

Glorious defeat, a fine English tradition, is often viewed as being preferable to hard-faced, pragmatic victory. Hunslet's standing in rugby league is, without doubt, higher because of their huge contribution to one of the finest matches in the sport's history than it would have been had they prevailed in the manner of their semi-final victory over Wakefield Trinity, following which *Wakefield Express* reporter John Allen opined, 'If similar procedure is followed by Hunslet, profitable as it might be, the Empire Stadium exit gangways will be crowded long before the finish of the final against Wigan.'

The result and the epic nature of the contest hinged on a disallowed try, in the thirteenth minute, for Welsh right-winger John Griffiths; the only non-Yorkshireman in a side that included two other non-locals, in scrum half Alan Marchant and open-side prop Dennis Hartley. Griffiths dived in at the corner from a pass by Hartley and when Warrington referee Joe Manley pointed to the spot the Parksiders, now 5-2 ahead and with full-back Billy Langton set to attempt the conversion attempt, would have taken some overhauling. In the days of unlimited tackles, and with hooker Bernard Prior rated as arguably the finest securer of possession in the game, Hunslet would simply have stuffed the ball up their jumpers and in all probability ground out a victory that, because of its manner, would have been no more popular beyond south Leeds than had been their success over Wakefield. However, in a moment that has prompted debate ever since the touch judge raised his flag. And to Hunslet's chagrin and Wigan's joy, the try was vetoed. The Parksiders, never again given the opportunity to take the lead, were forced to chase the game and duly played a full part in a classic.

That the pundits were surprised by the closeness of the final scoreline was in itself surprising. Hunslet boasted a side packed with past, present and future internationals and, until the turn of the year, had been riding high in the league table with only Wigan and St Helens above them. The Parksiders, diverted by the Wembley trail, lost their league form in the second half of the campaign and slumped to fourteenth in the table. But the quality within the squad remained undeniable. Langton was possibly the best uncapped full-back in the game, the powerful Griffiths finished with 26 tries that season, and his centre Geoff Shelton, who had played in both of Great Britain's games against France the previous year, was selected for the 1966 tour of Australia and went on to total 7 caps. Young second row Bill Ramsey joined Shelton on that tour and was to return to Wembley on four further occasions, with Leeds and Widnes, while stand-off Brian Gabbitas was a glittering talent and should have eared more than his solitary cap in 1959. Veteran Geoff Gunney, in fine form in the second row, had become an elder statesman of the game, while open-side prop Dennis Hartley, a buy from Doncaster a couple of years earlier, was to terrorise the Aussies on the 1970 Ashes-winning tour. Prior gained a Test cap in 1966, against France, while remaining players such as centre Alan Preece, blind-side prop Ken Eyre, winger Barry Lee and captain and loose forward Fred Ward were at least of county standard. Hunslet, therefore, had no reason to fear a Wigan outfit that,

---

Hunslet 16   Wigan 20

Beaten but unbowed: Barry Lee, Bernard Prior and Dennis Hartley acknowledge a rapturous reception from the crowd. In the background, Geoff Shelton and Alan Marchant chew over the 'ifs and buts'.

despite having been at Wembley in 1958, 1959, 1961 and 1963, had eight players making their first appearance at the Twin Towers.

The Parksiders were even undeterred by a catastrophic start, scrum half Alan Marchant sending the kick-off directly into touch and Wigan loose forward Laurie Gilfedder kicking the penalty from halfway. It was ironic that Marchant should have been at fault. The Featherstone-born scrum half had been snapped up from Halifax the previous September for £3,500 as a replacement for the aging Jeff Stevenson and his impact had been immediate, Hunslet winning their next seven games to rise to the upper reaches of the table. Within four minutes the Parksiders were on level terms, Langton landing a forty-five-yard penalty when Wigan second row Roy Evans obstructed Prior.

The full-back didn't get the chance to extend Hunslet's lead when Griffiths' try was vetoed and Wigan made the most of that escape when, three minutes later, Langton failed to find touch with a penalty; a recurring fault, shared with Gunney. Gilfedder and full-back Ray Ashby made the most of the opportunity, sending right centre Keith Holden over for an unconverted try. Langton and Gilfedder traded penalties before a crash tackle on Ward, Hunslet's playmaker, reduced his effectiveness and Preece, hero of the semi-final, spent half the game in a daze after having halted the great Wigan winger Billy Boston in full flight.

Hunslet, though, continued to adopt an expansive approach as did Wigan, primarily through the incisive attacking raids of Ashby. The Parksiders' key figure, with a potent mix of explosive and elusive skills, was Gabbitas and the pair were to share the Lance Todd Trophy as joint Men of

HUNSLET v. WIGAN

Prop Dennis Hartley fires out the pass that led to winger John Griffiths' disallowed try.

the Match although the *Yorkshire Post*'s Alfred Drewry was typically forthright. 'Ashby was full of enterprise and brought off one of the game's most spectacular coupes, but Shelton and Griffiths in turn showed up his defensive shortcomings when they scored Hunslet's two tries. Gabbitas, on the other hand, has never played better in all his long and distinguished career. Every time he got the ball he was a menace to the Wigan defence.'

John Bapty of the *Yorkshire Evening Post* enthused: 'Gabbitas was an off half with inspiration in his hands and feet almost every time he touched the ball. Shelton looked as good as a centre can when he moved in the middle with the ball; the forwards, with Gunney always on the job, with young Ramsey coming on mightily in the second half to tell of the future there is for him, with Eyre, Hartley, Ward and Prior doing their stuff, carried firmly the colours made famous by the "Terrible Six."'

Rhodesian winger Trevor Lake – another contender for the Lance Todd Trophy – raced over for his first try as half-time approached, courtesy of Holden's pass, and Gilfedder's third goal stretched the Pie Eaters' lead to eight points. Hunslet, though, provided a reminder of their tenacious approach with a blockbusting try from Shelton, who brushed aside four defenders after being given a glimmer of a chance by Gabbitas. Langton's conversion reduced the half-time deficit to a manageable 12-9 scoreline but a tendency to lose possession in promising positions again proved costly for the Parksiders early in the second period.

Brian McTigue and Evans were devastating in response, mounting an attack that led to Gilfedder racing over from forty-five yards despite the attentions of Shelton and Langton, his captain Eric Ashton successfully taking over the kicking duties. Hunslet had an escape when Holden had a try

Hunslet were in relaxed mood on the train to Wembley. Sharing a joke with Fred Ward and Alan Marchant (sitting) are (from left to right): Bernard Prior, Ken Eyre, Brian Gabbitas and Alan Preece.

The Hunslet Rugby League Parkside Players' Association, membership of which is limited to men who played for Hunslet prior to the sale of Parkside, is perhaps the most exclusive club in sport. A reunion is held annually on the first Sunday in June. Here, members of the 1965 Wembley squad line up. From left to right, back row: Geoff Shelton, Arthur Render, Geoff Gunney, Dennis Hartley, Ken Eyre, Fred Ward, John Griffiths, Bill Ramsey. Front row: Billy Baldwinson, Alan Marchant, Billy Langton, Alan Preece.

ruled out for double movement, while Langton was unable to reduce the arrears when a penalty attempt went astray. The Parksiders, however, suggested that victory against the odds was a real possibility with a spell of heavy pressure, but were to regret three instances in which possession was lost in promising situations. Ashby, from the last of those, swung the issue emphatically towards Wigan, racing past three defenders in a thirty-yard surge to feed Lake, who held off Griffiths in a thrilling chase to the corner to register one of Wembley Stadium's more scintillating scores. Gilfedder, unable to covert, was also wide with a subsequent penalty attempt but Hunslet, eleven points adrift, were not finished.

The Parksiders, with second-row pair Gunney and Ramsey in inspired mood, dominated the final quarter, coming close to staging one of the great fightbacks at the Twin Towers. Griffiths, a charismatic figure, popped up on the end of a passing movement to charge over from thirty yards for a richly deserved try, Langton converting, and there were real hopes of victory in the closing stages when Langton kicked a penalty with just four minutes left. Wigan, though, retained possession, ensuring that Hunslet's bid petered out. To Wigan, the glory and the silver. To Hunslet, merely the glory. But what glory after one of the finest contests in the history of sport!

Hunslet: Langton, Griffiths, Shelton, Preece, Lee, Gabbitas, Marchant, Hartley, Prior, Eyre, Ramsey, Gunney, Ward.

Wigan: Ashby, Boston, Ashton, Holden, Lake, Hill, Parr, Gardiner, Clarke, McTigue, Stephens, Evans, Gilfedder.

Hunslet v. Castleford

Date: 27 September 1965   Yorkshire Cup semi-final
Location: Parkside

The 1964/65 Challenge Cup runners-up made certain of a second appearance in a major final in the space of six months with a notable victory over the competition favourites. Castleford, who had last reached the Yorkshire Cup final in 1950 – losing to mighty Huddersfield – travelled to Parkside on the back of five successive wins against Yorkshire teams in the early weeks of the season and with most pundits predicting that that notable run would continue. Hunslet, bidding to retrieve a trophy they had last won three years earlier, were reeling from the loss of mercurial stand-off Brian Gabbitas, who would never play again after a facial injury sustained at Huddersfield at the beginning of the month. Welsh winger John Griffiths, a man who had been so loyal to the cause that he had spurned overtures from Leeds, was another absentee, having returned to the Valleys for what turned out to be a season-long sabbatical after a dispute with the directors.

The Parksiders had selected highly rated youngster Billy Hood – who had opted for his local side despite the temptation of a lucrative offer from Keighley – at stand-off in the previous three fixtures. Two of those, against Hull in the Yorkshire Cup, and at home to Leigh, had been won, but between times the trip to Keighley had ended in defeat. Hood was destined to make just one further first-team appearance; in the centre in the following season's Lazenby Cup fixture with Leeds.

Faced with the offensive threat of Castleford number six Alan Hardisty, Hunslet opted to switch pragmatic centre Alan Preece to stand-off, with hard-bitten Arthur Render taking his place. The pacey and elusive Tommy Thompson, a regular first choice a couple of seasons earlier, had been given another chance in the first team, which he would snatch with both hands.

The visitors lacked brilliant stand-off Alan Hardisty, who was replaced by Derek Edwards, with eighteen-year-old Roger Millward taking the left-wing berth. Johnny Walker, who would later replace Hunslet skipper Fred Ward, was in the second row.

The 9,753 midweek crowd witnessed a seesaw clash that would have graced the final. Only seven days earlier, several of the combatants had featured on the same side in Yorkshire's 15-8 victory over New Zealand in a match that celebrated the switching on of Castleford's floodlights. But temporary allegiances were forgotten as Hunslet appeared to assume control by the break, when a 7-0 lead had been established after a dominant first-half performance and a notable defensive display by scrum half Alan Marchant, who pulled off a series of try-saving tackles on Walker, prop Charlesworth and Hepworth. Those stops laid the platform from which the Parksiders, who had themselves been denied when Edwards thwarted second row Geoff Gunney and winger Barry Lee, established their interval advantage.

Full-back Billy Langton opened the home account with a penalty and Preece then gave Lee a tight chance that he took in style, using his solid frame to crash over in the corner. Langton added a magnificent conversion but, within five minutes of the restart, Castleford were in front, thanks to two tries by Millward who showed all the skills that had made him a firm favourite on ITV's pioneering Sunday morning show,

Hunslet 17   Castleford 10

Several Hunslet players starred for Yorkshire against New Zealand in the match that celebrated the switching on of the floodlights at Wheldon Road, Castleford, just seven days before the Yorkshire Cup semi-final. Both clubs regularly supplied a steady stream of players to the county side. Pictured in another Yorkshire line-up of the era (all on the back row) are: Dennis Hartley (third from left), Bill Ramsey (fifth from left) and Geoff Shelton (seventh from left). Former Hunslet captain Harry Poole (with ball) captained the side. Castleford players pictured include Bill Bryant (between Ramsey and Shelton) and, on the front row, Alan Hardisty, Keith Hepworth and Derek Edwards.

which featured top junior games. His first, almost from the kick-off, stemmed from fine approach work by second row Bill Bryant and Charlesworth, hooker Johnny Ward using his deft handling skills to send the youngster between Langton and Lee. Millward converted his own score from the touchline and was quickly back on the scoresheet, leaving Hunslet floundering after a timely Edwards pass. This time, though he couldn't convert – and the remainder of the match was to belong to Hunslet.

The Parksiders hit back in the fifty-fourth minute when Bill Ramsey broke through to send prop Ken Eyre over at the posts. Langton retrieved the lead with his conversion and stretched Hunslet's advantage with a penalty, but Millward ensured that Castleford remained in the frame when he reduced the deficit to four points with his second goal. Marchant, however, pulled off a mighty cover tackle on Millward, who had a clear run to the line, which effectively sealed a match in which Gunney was another key figure. It was Lee, a relatively unsung hero in a fine Hunslet side, who sealed the Parksiders' trip to Headingley and a final with the newly reformed Bradford Northern. The winger, again given a chance out wide, made no mistake, squeezing past a posse of defenders for what turned out to be the clinching score.

Millward, meanwhile, had made a huge impression despite being on the beaten side. Ironically, the young star spent the rest of the evening in the area, allowing the team coach to return to Castleford without him and joining his future wife Carol – a Hunslet lass – with her father Walter in the Anchor, the pub run by former Parkside half-back Jeff Stevenson, before catching the bus home.

Hunslet: Langton, Lee, Shelton, Render, Thompson, Preece, Marchant, Hartley, Prior, Eyre, Ramsey, Gunney, Ward.

Castleford: Bedford, Howe, C. Battye, M. Battye, Millward, Edwards, Hepworth, Terry, Ward, Charlesworth, Walker, Bryant, Taylor.

BRADFORD NORTHERN v. HUNSLET

Date: 16 October 1965

Location: Headingley

Yorkshire Cup final

Referee: Mr W.E. Lawrinson (Warrington)

Hunslet, hot favourites to recover the Yorkshire Cup after a three-year gap, were subjected to a stunning defeat that, other than in south Leeds, was universally popular throughout the sporting world.

The Parksiders, themselves the darlings of the rugby league public after their glorious display against Wigan at Wembley a little over five months earlier, were upstaged by a Northern club that had been reformed only twelve months earlier after having collapsed in late 1963. Trevor Foster, Joe Phillips and others had cobbled together a side that captured the imaginations of fans within and without Bradford.

Rival clubs, keen to see Northern back in action, had let decent players move to Odsal, invariably at bargain prices, and the reborn Bradford had reached their first final on the back of a euphoric tide. With former Huddersfield captain Tommy Smales, who had won the championship with Fartown in 1962, on board, Northern had opened the campaign with six league wins from nine games and a memorable 28-15 victory over the touring Kiwis. They had, awhile, accounted for Keighley and Hull KR respectively in the opening rounds of the Yorkshire Cup before drawing Huddersfield at the semi-final stage. The claret & golds looked to have done enough after drawing 7-7 at Odsal but Northern produced a mature display just twenty-four hours later in the replay to win 7-4 and delight their manager Gus Risman by booking a date at Headingley with Hunslet.

Few outside Bradford expected anything other than a victory for the Parksiders. Hunslet, indeed, had the better of the match territorially but without the presence of stand-off Brian Gabbitas, who had been forced to retire after having his jaw broken in a late tackle the previous month in a game at Huddersfield, struggled to turn their dominance into points. Northern, by contrast, won the game through two tries scored from close to their own line, each registered after heavy spells of Parkside pressure.

Former Wakefield Trinity centre Ian Brooke grabbed the first, notching a sensational touchdown out of nothing in a remarkable seventy-five-yard sprint in which a number of would-be tacklers were left sprawling. Prop Terry Clawson, a capture from Featherstone Rovers, kicked the goal and a penalty to give Bradford a surprise seven-point lead for the 17,522 crowd – the best for a Yorkshire Cup final since Hunslet's appearance three years earlier and one that would not be bettered until Hull and Hull KR met at Boothferry Park in 1984 – to reflect upon.

Hunslet's supporters had their worries eased when centre Geoff Shelton powered over but the fates, again, were not with the Parksiders as Northern took a grip with a match-winning touchdown for stand-off Dave Stockwell. The half back, far from the fastest man on the pitch, appeared to pose no great threat when he broke the first line of defence deep in his own half. But with a mesmerising mix of feints, dummies, half-shimmies and swerves, he somehow managed to progress sixty yards.

Bradford Northern 17   Hunslet 8

Bradford Northern *v.* Hunslet

The fates conspired against odds-on favourites Hunslet in the 1965 Yorkshire Cup final. Elusive left winger Tommy Thompson, who later joined Bradford, gives the Parksiders some respite with a well-taken try.

With Hunslet finally threatening to bring him down, Stockwell flung out a pass to Australian winger Lionel Williamson who crossed in the corner for try that sent Northern cheerleader Diane Rhodes, who would later marry the Aussie and leave with him for his homeland, into delight.

Stung, Hunslet again rallied. Tommy Thompson, who would subsequently move to Odsal, rounded off one of the Parksiders' few incisive moves to squeeze in by the flag. But the gods were with Bradford and Smales made certain of the cup, working a blind-side move at a scrum to put Williamson in for his second touchdown. Bradford supporters raced onto the pitch to acclaim their heroes, while Hunslet, again disappointed having been favourites, returned to south Leeds unaware that their side would not again feature in a major final. Northern, however, having worked so hard to win some silverware, turned out to be a shade careless while the Yorkshire Cup was in their care. The Odsal outfit managed to lose the trophy – twice. On each occasion, club officials were relieved when it resurfaced undamaged. The cup first went missing during a function at the Queens Hall, Bradford, in the month following their victory. Risman had left it in his boot during the event and there were furrowed brows when he later found that his car had been broken into. But there were relieved smiles when the trophy was found behind a wall.

Northern were equally fortunate the following August, although Leeds were not too happy. Bradford, having won the 1966 Leeds Sevens, granted their supporters' club permission to display the two trophies at a presentation night. The supporters' club secretary, garaging his car on returning home, left the Yorkshire Cup in his boot and the Sevens Trophy on the back seat. He was shocked the next morning to find that his garage had been broken into and his car stolen. The vehicle was recovered later in the day with the boot unlocked but with the Yorkshire Cup undamaged. The Sevens Trophy, though, had vanished without trace.

Bradford Northern: Scattergood, Williamson, Brooke, Rhodes, Walker, Stockwell, Smales, Tonkinson, Morgan, Hill, Ashton, Clawson, Rae.

Hunslet: Langton, Lee, Shelton, Render, Thompson, Preece, Marchant, Hartley, Prior, Eyre, Ramsey, Gunney, Ward.

HUNSLET v. YORK

Date: 21 April 1973
Location: Parkside

League
Referee: Mr G. Wilson (Dewsbury)

The curtain came down on eighty-five years of professional rugby league at Parkside with a sixth successive defeat for Hunslet in the penultimate match of the season. The game wasn't the last played by the old Hunslet club – that came two days later with the 15-8 defeat at the Barley Mow against Bramley – nor was it the last match at Parkside, as an amateur fixture subsequently took place on the famous old ground before the bulldozers moved in.

Effectively, however, the fixture with York on 21 April 1973 was the end of a mainly glorious era and, finishing as it did in defeat, echoed the preceding four months in which just one league game – at home to Doncaster on 10 March, 14-13 – had been won. That apart, Hunslet's only other victory in a desultory close had been in the first round of the Challenge Cup in January, when amateurs Millom had made the Parksiders work hard for an 18-5 win in Cumbria. Just four matches had finished in victory prior to Christmas; at home to Blackpool Borough (20-11) and Workington Town (19-18) and by 26-10 when Huyton were entertained at Parkside, with a fairly merry Christmas evoked with the 24 December verdict at Doncaster, the 11-6 success presaging a rare 'double'. The Dons, though, still managed to finish ahead of the Parksiders in the table, by two points. Remarkably, Hunslet could point to some improvement in their last season, finishing third from bottom – above Blackpool Borough and Huyton – to avoid a third successive acquaintance with the wooden spoon.

Geoff Gunney, a stalwart of the side for twenty-four years, was the last man to leave the pitch in a highly moving cameo that would have been even more emotional had the players and the supporters known the truth; that Hunslet RLFC would be no more. Hunslet's directors had insisted, during the sale of Parkside to property developers, that plans were in hand for a new stadium. The *Yorkshire Evening Post*'s Arthur Haddock wrote, the night before the game: 'As the bulldozers prepare to roar into action, smash down the old pavilion and level the area, and the steel erectors start building the vast warehousing complex earmarked for the site, a short distance away work will soon be starting on a new home for the club.

'Much work has to be accomplished in the sixteen weeks before the start of next season to knock into shape the virgin site between the M1 and Middleton Road, near Woodhouse Hill Cemetery, that Leeds Corporation are providing as the new ground.

'The irony of all this is that Hunslet are going back from whence they came, for it was from Woodhouse Hill, due to the demands of a grasping landlord, that the pioneers moved to Parkside and virtually carved out the place from the rubble and a 2,000-ton slagheap.'

In the event the directors failed to secure a new ground and Hunslet RFLC duly folded at the end of 1972/73. A crowd of 700, paying £200, gathered in a funereal atmosphere for a game which followed the depressing pattern of most Hunslet games of the preceding three or four seasons.

Hunslet 5   York 22

A poignant moment as the long-serving Geoff Gunney becomes the last man to lead out a Hunslet team at Parkside.

Loose forward Phil Sanderson, assisted by prop Ronnie Dobson and scrum half Phil Horrocks, sparked an early raid that led to prop Billy Adams going close with a penalty attempt, but York turned the tables with a counterattack in which prop Malcolm Dixon sent stand-off Gary Smith over from forty yards for centre Steve Quinn to convert. Hunslet centre George Clark was denied by a tackle by York full-back Keith Gullen, and Horrocks went close, before another breakaway try – this time by winger Mick Major, who popped up on the end of a combination involving loose forward Danny Sheehan and centre Dave Rippon – plus Quinn's fine conversion put the Minstermen in the driving seat. There were strong signs of the old Parkside spirit, though, when Dobson crashed over, Adams' conversion reducing the deficit to five points.

York, however, assumed firm control in the second period. Bidding to secure a spot in the following season's top flight as the RFL repeated its earlier experiment with two divisions, the visitors edged further ahead when Dixon landed a drop goal from thirty-five yards. And, despite the brave efforts of such as Geoff Gunney – playing at full-back – second row Ken Sykes, and winger Jack Richardson, yet another defeat in front of a crowd that included former players Johnny Place (1925 to 1929), Cyril Morrell (1921 to 1947) and Frank 'Dolly' Dawson (1921 to 1937) could not be avoided. Welsh winger Clive Hill went over to stretch York's lead and, as time began to run out on eighty minutes of rugby and ninety years of history, Major grabbed his second try and Quinn kicked two more goals.

Gunney, whose seventy-two-year-old mother Rosie was serving tea on the day, just as she had for the previous fifteen years, said: 'I am heartbroken.' He wasn't alone.

Hunslet: Gunney, Watson, G. Clark, Barron, Richardson, Rycroft, Horrocks, Dobson, J. Clark, Adams, Sykes, Griffiths, Sanderson. Subs: Charlton, Taylor.

York: Gullen, Hill, Rippon, Quinn, Major, Smith, Sullivan, Dixon, Payne, Forsyth, Dunham, Hillman, Sheehan. Subs: Meillam, Cookland.

NEW HUNSLET v. HUYTON

Date: 26 August 1973   Division Two
Location: Leeds Greyhound Stadium   **Referee:** Mr P. Massey (Salford)

A little over four short months after Hunslet's last game at Parkside, a reborn club opened competitive life with a comfortable, if fractious, victory over their fellow strugglers of the previous few seasons.

Promises by the former board of a new ground had come to nothing and Hunslet legend Geoff Gunney, together with men such as Ronnie Teeman and Gordon Murray, toiled tirelessly to ensure that the old Parkside spirit would not be allowed to slip quietly away. The stalwarts had the support of the Rugby Football League, which asked all other clubs to abide by a 'gentleman's agreement' not to sign any of the former Hunslet players. The legality of that edict was, however, questioned by several of the leading lights of the old Parkside squad. Young stand-off Bob Gaitley was a target of Oldham, who reluctantly agreed to adhere to the RFL's ruling, leaving his registration at headquarters at Chapeltown Road and still playing the Townville product in a pre-season friendly. Captain David Marshall, recognised as one of the best full-backs in the game, took legal advice and signed for Leeds, where he was joined by rangy packman Phil Sanderson. And free-scoring centre George Clarke, after playing in the first game against Huyton, went on to Hull.

Most of the old squad, however, led by such as Barry Lee, Ken Sykes, Alan Griffiths, Phil Horrocks and Jack Richardson, remained loyal to the cause. The new directors, meanwhile, had secured tenancy at the Greyhound Stadium, opposite Leeds United's Elland Road ground. The stadium would gain certain notoriety for the narrowness of its pitch and for the goalposts, in the style of a TV aerial and unique in rugby league, which rested on one post placed on the dead-ball line rather than on the try line. That feature would often unsettle opposing teams and one player – Oldham's Mike Elliott – actually missed out on scoring what would have been a crucial try, glancing across to the posts as he raced over the goal line and touching down beyond the dead ball line in error. The incident led to criss-cross markings being painted in the in-goal area to prevent further confusion. Timekeeper Barry Sirrs subsequently shed further light on the incident. He said: 'The wingman dived over the dead ball line because our full-back Bob Pickles was stood on the dead ball line to make the last tackle, so naturally Elliott on seeing this dived past him and over the dead ball line, thinking it was the try line. We could of course give Bob the benefit of the doubt and suggest that this was a new defensive tactic thought up between him and Paul Daley.'

The fledgling club was, appropriately, called 'New Hunslet' and, after a friendly at Keighley that ended in an honourable 19-10 defeat, the new side, wearing all white (subsequently white with a green 'V') was ready for serious action. The Hunslet directors laid on special buses throughout the first season or two to help supporters from the Hunslet, Belle Isle and Middleton areas get to the ground and that initiative paid off immediately, a crowd of 4,500 turning up for a highly charged, emotional occasion.

New Hunslet 23   Huyton 0

New Hunslet v. Huyton

Second row Ken Sykes enjoyed a well-deserved benefit with Hunslet in the late 1970s. Memories of the first match at Elland Road provided a focal point of the celebrations.

The first match at Elland Road

DATE — AUGUST 26th 1973
OPPONENTS — HUYTON
SCORE — NEW HUNSLET 23   HUYTON 0
ATTENDANCE — 4,500

TEAMS

NEW HUNSLET		HUYTON
1. G. NICHOLS		1. LLOYD
2. B. LEE		2. LEATHERBARROW
3. G. CLARK		3. THOMPSON
4. S. BARRON		4. BOURNE
5. J. RICHARDSON	REFEREE	5. WESTHEAD
6. P. RYCROFT	P. A. Massey	6. NUTTALL
7. P. HORROCKS		7. PRESCOTT
8. D. WATSON		8. GOULDING
9. D. TEESDALE		9. NEWTON
10. M. JOHNSON		10. WAGSHAW
11. F. PICKUP		11. WILLIAMS
12. K. SYKES		12. PARRY
13. A. GRIFFITHS		13. WILLS
14. C. WATSON		14.
15. R. DOBSON		15.

The New Hunslet scorers in this Match were:

G. NICHOLS   7 Goals   1 Try
B. LEE   1 Try
G. CLARK   1 Try

G. GUNNEY   D. WATSON   F. PICKUP   A. GRIFFITHS   G. CLARK
R. DOBSON   M. JOHNSON   K. SYKES   J. RICHARDSON

C. WATSON   P. RYCROFT   D. TEESDALE   S. BARRON
B. LEE   P. HORROCKS   G. NICHOLS

Among them was Bobby Collins, the diminutive former captain of Leeds United, who performed a ceremonial kick-off, and there was a further connection with the soccer club in the early stages of New Hunslet's tenancy. The Greyhound Stadium naturally lacked changing facilities for human beings and United helped their new neighbours by opening up their changing rooms. It was confirmed against Huyton that dressing rooms within the Greyhound Stadium were a necessity, not a luxury. In an abrasive game, three players were dismissed in the closing quarter. Horrocks was given his marching orders, together with Huyton number seven David Prescott and captain and loose forward Keith Wills, but those incidents had no bearing on a result that delighted Hunslet's long-suffering supporters.

Full-back Geoff Nicholls, back with his former club after a spell with Leeds, was in impressive form and totalled seventeen points with a try and seven goals. Lee also crossed the whitewash, and his centre George Clark grabbed New Hunslet's other try. Fred Pickup, who had played in Leeds' championship side of twelve years earlier, had been enticed from north of the river and was a seminal figure in the pack.

The important factor, however, beyond the result and its nature, was that a professional team was alive and representing Hunslet. Mr Ronnie Simpson, the chairman of the Rugby Football League, was among the chief guests and he enthused: 'I think it's a wonderful opening for a club which was only started a month ago. I never visualised anything like this and it should certainly encourage the officials and players.'

Hunslet's Steve Barron was certainly encouraged. Ronnie Teeman, delighted by the big crowd and the £1,180 takings, immediately handed over a cheque for £250 to the centre, honouring the terms of Barron's contract with the old club.

New Hunslet: Nicholls, Lee, Clark, Barron, Richardson, Rycroft, Horrocks, Watson, Teasdale, Dobson, Johnstone, Sykes, Griffiths. Subs: Riggs, Williams.

Huyton: Lloyd, Leatherbarrow, Thompson, Bourne, Westhead, Nuttall, Prescott, Goulaing, Newton, Wagshaw, Williams, Parry, Wills.

New Hunslet v. Widnes

Date: 23 October 1974

Location: Leeds Greyhound Stadium

BBC2 Floodlit Trophy

Referee: Mr S. Wall (Leigh)

Any doubts Geoff Gunney and his colleagues my have harboured over the wisdom of forming the new club were surely dispelled when New Hunslet, in only their second season, added to the celebrations surrounding the switching on of their new £4,000 floodlights by pulling off an amazing victory over what was undoubtedly one of the best teams in the game. Widnes, who would finish fifth in Division One – in stark contrast to New Hunslet's eleventh in Division Two – were the acclaimed 'Cup Kings' of the Rugby League. The Chemics would go on to win the Challenge Cup later in the season, overcoming derby rivals Warrington (who reached Wembley via a third round victory over New Hunslet at a packed Greyhound Stadium), and would also feature at Wembley the following year, going down to St Helens. Widnes also reached the John Player Trophy final in 1974/75 and, a matter of only ten days after their defeat at Hunslet, were to beat reigning champions Salford 6-2 in the Lancashire Cup final.

Coach Paul Daley, faced with such opposition, could perhaps have been forgiven for asking for little more from his charges than an honourable showing in inevitable defeat. Daley, however, had never been a player in a glittering career with Halifax and Bradford to anticipate anything other than victory, and he carried the same philosophy into his coaching. His players responded in wonderful style against a Widnes outfit that had not previously lost away from home that season. A tremendous defensive display, in which second-row forward Jimmy Crampton put in a typically heroic tackling stint before being compelled to withdraw with an accidentally broken nose, was complemented by an exhibition of efficient goal-kicking by Geoff Nicholls. The full-back scored the only points of the first half with four long-range penalties and New Hunslet were never diverted thereafter. Widnes were still capable of mounting an effective rescue operation but their prospects realistically vanished six minutes into the second period. Speedy centre George Clark was the destroyer, ending the Chemics' hopes with an audacious interception before racing away over seventy yards. Clark had, however, to utilise more than mere speed to register the score. Widnes full-back Ray Dutton, among the best defenders in the game and the holder of 6 Great Britain caps, represented a serious obstacle but the New Hunslet centre was up to the task, holding off the 1970 World Cup man's challenge to secure one of the most important touchdowns in his career.

Prop Geoff Crewdson, centre Steve Barron, loose forward Alan Griffiths, hooker Alan Maskill and scrum half Phil Horrocks were among the leading lights as Hunslet continued to deny a roused Widnes, and the chances of a major upset improved to the point of near-certainty when stand-off Bob Gaitley kicked a drop goal. The Chemics' response, when it came, was too little and too late. Second row Mick Adams scored their only try, ten minutes from time, and added the conversion. New Hunslet, however, held out for a memorable win, the finest in the club's short history, to secure a second round tie at Warrington. In the programme notes

New Hunslet 12   Widnes 5

An early New Hunslet line-up. From left to right, back row: Stan Whittaker, Tommy Taylor, Jimmy Crampton, Geoff Crewdson, Fred Pickup, Alan Maskill, Don Watson, Ken Sykes. Front row: Chris Mowforth, Jack Richardson, Geoff Fisher, Phil Horrocks, Geoff Nicholls, Bob Gaitley, Morgan.

for the following home fixture with Doncaster the club enthused: 'Whether it was playing in the Celtic colours of Green and White that fired our team or whether it was because the lights shine only on the worthy we do not know but if any supporter could have forecast such a win then he or she is a supreme optimist.

'No one could be under any illusion that the task was anything other than colossal. Trevor Watson of the *Yorkshire Evening Post* said that he had never seen a better tackling display than that of our team and of Jimmy Crampton in particular. There was no unsavoury incident in the match; it was well controlled by a young referee, Mr Wall of Leigh, who we are sure a lot more will be heard of in the future.

'The atmosphere was electric and the scenes around the dressing room after the match quite amazing. Little Bobby Collins, who performed the ceremony of switching on the lights and in his honour we played in his beloved Celtic strip, said afterwards that he thought that many thousands were present because of the noise the supporters made.'

Unfortunately, they were the only people privileged to witness a magnificent display in a competition created purely for TV. The program notes continued: 'Of all the matches played in the first round of this tournament the outstanding match was New Hunslet v. Widnes, which was one of the three that were not televised. Once can forgive the BBC for thinking that this would be an uneven combat but when one saw the massacre of Leeds by St Helens on the television the BBC must be sorry that they underestimated New Hunslet.'

New Hunslet: Nicholls, Fisher, Clark, Barron, Hudson, Gaitley, Horrocks, Crewdson, Maskill, Watson, Crampton, Chawner, Griffiths. Sub: Sykes.

Widnes: Dutton, George, O'Neill, Laughton, Anderson, Hughes, Bowden, Stephens, Elwell, Sheridan, Adams, Blackwood, Peek. Subs: Warburton, Foran.

Hunslet v. Hull Kingston Rovers

Date: 13 February 1983
Location: Elland Road

Challenge Cup first round
Referee: Mr M.R. Whitfield (Widnes)

The glory of the Challenge Cup resides in its ability to produce the greatest of contests between the best club teams in the game, combined with an abiding capacity to produce the unexpected. No sport can consider itself healthy if results become foregone conclusions. The lifeblood of a team game such as rugby league rests in the quality of matches between sides in the upper echelons, and in its facility to emit, from time to time, a match such as the one that took place in mid-February 1983.

Had Valentine's Day fallen on the Sunday, rather than the following day, journalists at Elland Road – Hunslet's home since the previous summer, following a spell at Mount Pleasant, Batley – would have been preparing for a report along the lines of the famous gangland massacre in Chicago. There was, simply, no way in the world that Hunslet could overcome the Robins.

Hull KR, after all, were aristocrats. Rovers had appeared at Wembley two years earlier, losing to Widnes after having beaten neighbours Hull the previous season, and were to be back at the Twin Towers in 1986 for a tilt with Castleford. The Robins would finish the campaign in second place in Division One and, twelve months later, would secure both the championship and the Premiership. Rovers were also in the middle of a period in which regular appearances were made in the Yorkshire Cup final and the Regal Trophy final. Coached by Roger Millward, Hull Kingston Rovers were second favourites to win the 1982/83 Challenge Cup; and a glance through their line-up suggested that the rating was fully justified. Full-back George Fairburn was just one of many internationals in the side. Others who had either played for Great Britain in the past or who would do so in the future included winger Gary Clark, centre Mike Smith, stand-off Steve Hartley, hooker David Watkinson, second row Phil Lowe and loose forward Len Casey; while scrum half Gordon Smith was a current New Zealand international and had topped the Kiwis' points-scoring list on the previous summer's tour of Australia. The power and strength-in-depth of the Robins was further illustrated by the fact that two more Great Britain men, Chris Burton and Andy Kelly, were on the bench; and two further internationals, Phil Hogan and New Zealander Gary Prohm, were unavailable because of dispute and injury respectively. Hunslet's prospects against that line-up were, in the eyes of the pundits and all but the more starry-eyed of their supporters, nil.

Hunslet's players took a different view and, led by veteran loose forward Johnny Wolford (a huge talent and one of the most intelligent, inventive and skilful players to have been involved in the sport, either with hand or boot), they were right. The south Leeds outfit had several other players in their ranks of high quality. Graham King, a scrum half blessed with blistering speed and more than his fair share of talent, was of international class and a superb support player who benefited regularly from Wolford's promptings. Stewart Smith, dynamic in the second row, was also alert to Wolford's half breaks while Hunslet had other hard-running and strong-tackling forwards in New

Hunslet 12   Hull KR 11

HUNSLET v. HULL KINGSTON ROVERS

A rare shot of master tactician Johnny Wolford with the ball under his arm. Wolford, the supreme creator, typically carried the ball in two hands and was rarely caught in possession. The maestro opted for safety first in this incident in the quarter-final against Castleford.

Four key players in Hunslet's shock win over Hull KR were livewire scrum half Graham King, orchestrator-in-chief Johnny Wolford, second row Stewart Smith and full-back Paul Briers. Here, Wolford receives the ball from King in the quarter-final tie with Castleford. Briers and Smith hover in anticipation of yet another masterly piece of creation by the veteran loose forward.

Zealander Jon Ackland and Geoff Wright. Props Mark Burgess and Neil Lean, meanwhile, were forceful and direct, while the side had a strong-tackling hooker in Phil Gibson who earned his side its fair share of the ball. Coach Paul Daley, an articulate and perceptive motivator, had enlisted an enterprising and tough-tackling stand-off from New Zealand in Glen Townsend, and he had also assembled a three-quarter line in which centres Peter Roe (virtually playing on one leg in his twilight years) and Bryan Murrell had acres of experience at the very highest level, with Bradford Northern and Leeds respectively. Outside them the likes of Kevin Olbison and Billy Foley impressed on the right while left-winger Eric Fitzsimons had become a key figure, primarily for his high-quality goal-kicking. Paul Briers, at the rear, was the epitome of the safe and dependable full-back, secure under the high kick, effective in the tackle, and possessed of wide vision in attack, while substitute Dean Booth was the kind of enthusiastic utility man that any coach is delighted to have on board. For all their undoubted qualities, however, Hunslet had failed to set Division Two alight and were to finish in sixth spot, well outside the promotion placings.

A healthy enough crowd of 4,441 ambled through the Elland Road turnstiles prepared for a run-of-the-mill, one-sided cup tie as the first stage of what would be Hull KR's serious attempt at the cup and league 'double'. They were to be privileged to witness one of the biggest – perhaps the

The Hunslet squad that graced Elland Road in the mid-1980s.

Opposite page: Centre Peter Roe, scorer of Hunslet's try, in typical barnstorming action. Johnny Wolford and Graham King are in support.

biggest – upsets in Challenge Cup history, and certainly the most serious shock to Hull KR's system since their 7-5 first round defeat at Batley in 1965 after they had been runners-up the previous year. Hunslet's victory was, however, richly deserved, even though the Robins scored two tries to one, and even allowing for the fact that Fairbairn could have snatched the spoils for Rovers if he had been successful with a penalty attempt from halfway.

Daley's charges laid the platform for victory in the first half when a phenomenally strong defensive performance limited Hull's options. Townsend harried poor Hartley all afternoon, with the result that the Robins' much-vaunted backline failed to click. Hunslet had one piece of good fortune when Clarke, put clear, sustained hamstring trouble and was halted by King, but there was no element of good fortune about the magnificent cover tackle that King subsequently executed on Phil Lowe when the fast-striding second row was heading for a certain try. The home side, on the back of those tackles and a goal and a drop by Fitzsimons went in at half-time at 3-3, Rovers having posted an Ian Robinson try. And the feeling was dawning among Hunslet supporters that possibly, just possibly, a real upset could be on the cards. That feeling gathered momentum when Wright broke through early in the second half and found Roe on his shoulder. The centre, running on sheer guts, empty and one leg, raced over from forty metres, Fitzsimons improving to edge Hunslet further in front. The ploy of bringing Fitzsimons in from the wing for drop goal attempts proved effective in the final quarter. The former Oldham flyer twice landed one-pointers to extend his side's lead to six points, with time ticking away. Fitzsimons, though, gave himself, his teammates, Daley and the fans a huge scare as the match drew to a close. Rovers, in a last-ditch effort, grabbed a try by Steve Hartley at the side of the posts. Fairburn added the extras to reduce the deficit to a single point but the electronic clock indicted that there was merely time for the restarting kick-off, and nothing more. Fitzsimons, however, agonisingly put too much beef into the ball, which sailed straight over the dead-ball line.

HUNSLET v. HULL KINGSTON ROVERS

Hull KR had an unexpected lifeline. Fairbairn placed the ball carefully on the centre spot and stepped back amid a crescendo of total silence. Three or four strides later, in what seemed like slow motion, the ball was heading high towards Hunslet's posts, but his gallant effort lacked sufficient accuracy. His shot drifted wide, and Hunslet had survived. An incredible result stunned the rest of the rugby league world in a round of shocks, with holders Widnes going out at home to Leeds. Other surprises were at Salford, where the Division Two outfit beat reigning champions Leigh 12-5, and in the clash of Division One sides at Oldham where Workington, who had been previously limited to only three wins, prevailed 8-5. Castleford upset the applecart with a 17-7 verdict at Central Park against Wigan but the reality was that no result elsewhere came close to matching the sheer audacity of Hunslet's victory over mighty Hull KR.

Hunslet were drawn at home to another Division One side in the next round in the shape of a Halifax outfit battling against relegation. The surprise, this time, would have been if Paul Daley's men had lost. In the event the side won 17-8, before 4,130 fans, to raise the idea that a trip to Wembley might, just might, be a real possibility.

Hunslet: Briers, Foley, Murrell, Roe, Fitzsimons, Townsend, King, Lean, Gibson, Burgess, S. Smith, Ackland, Wolford. Subs: Booth, Wright.

Hull KR: Fairburn, Clark, M. Smith, Robinson, Procter, Hartley, G. Smith, Millington, Watkinson, Crooks, Lowe, Casey. Subs: Burton, Kelly.

Hunslet v. Castleford

Date: 13 March 1983
Location: Elland Road

Challenge Cup third round
Referee: Mr M.R. Whitfield (Widnes)

A crowd of 14,004 witnessed an epic Challenge Cup tie played in rainswept conditions in which Hunslet emerged beaten but with pride fully intact.

Division One outfit Castleford, unarguably the better side, duly progressed to the semi-finals but Division Two Hunslet could justifiably argue that with a shade of luck they themselves could have found themselves at the penultimate stage for the first time in eighteen years. The south Leeds side, who maintained the pressure on Castleford until the very end, had the game's major figure in veteran Johnny Wolford while speedy scrum half Graham King was a perennial threat to the favourites. So, too, was New Zealand second row John Ackland, who with a touch of better fortune could have had a better return from a series of pinpoint kicks. The second row tested Castleford full-back Darren Coen with a series of testing bombs and, on all five occasions, Hunslet had several players in close attendance in anticipation of a slip. Coen succeeded in defusing two of the 'bombs.' Three, though, went astray; but, to Coen's evident relief and the home side's dismay, the ball either went dead each time or fell into the hands of a defender. The *Yorkshire Evening Post*'s Trevor Watson reported: 'Call them missed chances, call it bad luck, either way that's how cup ties are decided and it proved not to be Hunslet's day.'

Other than the result itself, Hunslet had plenty to be satisfied about, not least the huge gate as rugby league fans, sensing the possibility of a major upset, descended on Elland Road in their droves. Hunslet's last appearance in the quarter-finals had been in 1975, when Alex Murphy's Warrington, eventual finalists, had dampened the home camp's euphoria with a comfortable 23-3 victory at a sold-out Greyhound Stadium. That win had rarely been in doubt but, eight years later, Hunslet were to be in firm contention throughout against a Castleford side that was to feature as losing semi-finalists in three out of four years. A hard-fought match was contested in a fine spirit, with only four penalties awarded in a first half in which the visitors were clearly shaken by the enthusiastic and confident approach of their hosts.

Castleford struggled to get into gear, with uncertain handling in the face of the difficult conditions and the wholehearted approach of Hunslet's defenders. And it took the no-nonsense prop Kevin Ward, with a series of blockbusting charges, to settle the hot favourites. Ward too often lacked support but the occasion was one that demanded sheer hard graft rather than panache and twins Kevin and Bob Beardmore were at the forefront of Castleford's success. The silky skilled John Joyner also set a lead for the visitors with several important cover tackles, but he was unable to match the class of Wolford who, Trevor Watson enthused, 'provided all of 57 varieties with his dummies, short kicks, back flips... anything to keep the visitors on edge.'

Hunslet, with hooker Phil Gibson, prop Mark Burgess and Ackland prominent up front in defence, also had stifling presences out wide in the shape of centres Peter Roe and Bryan Murrell, while Paul Briers was coolness itself at the rear. Stewart Smith was a massive figure, showing pace in attack and commitment in defence before being forced to retire in the second period with double vision,

---

Hunslet 8   Castleford 13

Second row forward Stewart Smith charges over for Hunslet's try. Castleford's John Kear can only watch helplessly.

and it was the second row who crossed off Briers' clever pass to help Hunslet to a 6-5 interval lead. But Castleford confirmed their pedigree in the second period, adding two tries to their first-half score, with Bob Beardmore landing a second goal. That effort, and the touchdowns by right centre Tony Marchant, loose forward Andy Timson and left centre Gary Hyde, left brave Hunslet contemplating a hurdle that was just a shade too high.

The south Leeds side remained in contention with a penalty by their first round match-winner, winger Eric Fitzsimons, who had converted Smith's first-half touchdown in addition to kicking a drop goal. But Castleford held on, deservedly if a touch fortuitously, for one of the harder-earned victories in their Challenge Cup history. The abiding memory, meanwhile, is of the big crowd that, to a man or woman, could not fail to have been impressed by Hunslet's courageous display. The gate was significantly higher than the one recorded for the semi-final at Headingley the following month, when 10,784 turned up for the meeting of Bradford Northern and eventual cup winners Featherstone Rovers, who continued the tradition in the 1982/83 competition of upsets with a wonderful win over Hull in a contest in which the bookies had stopped accepting bets.

Castleford, meanwhile, returned to Elland Road for their own semi-final. Hunslet, as the host club, benefited from a share of takings of £65,498 from a 26,031 attendance. But crowds for their four remaining home league fixtures were disappointing. The attendances at the matches with Rochdale Hornets, York and Blackpool were, respectively, 802, 525 and 781, while 715 turned up for the game with Swinton, which was switched to Crown Flatt, Dewsbury.

Hunslet: Briers, Foley, Murrell, Roe, Fitzsimons, Townsend, King, Lean, Gibson, Burgess, S. Smith, Ackland, Wolford. Subs: Booth, Wright.

Castleford: Coen, Richards, Marchant, Hyde, Kear, Joyner, R. Beardmore, Connell, K. Beardmore, Johnson, James, Ward, Timson. Subs: Higgins, England.

LEIGH v. HUNSLET

Date: 27 February 1985
Location: Hilton Park, Leigh

Challenge Cup second round
Referee: Mr C. Hodgson (Maryport)

Few characters in English rugby league, if any, have more experience of the Challenge Cup, and more knowledge of what it takes to succeed in the competition, than Alex Murphy. The all-time great was centrally involved at Wembley on eight occasions. He was at stand-off for St Helens in 1961, when rivals Wigan were beaten 12-6, and captained the side to a 21-2 verdict from the centre when the teams met again in the decider five years later. Murphy was player-coach when Leigh accounted for Leeds 24-7 in 1971, and had a similar role when Warrington missed out 14-7 to Widnes in 1975. After hanging up his boots, he enjoyed further success as an out-and-out coach, taking Wigan to Wembley in 1984 and St Helens in 1987 and 1989.

Few of his experiences, however, will have matched that on 27 February 1985. Murphy, newly installed as Leigh coach after having left Wigan, was expected by the club and the fans to revive a Challenge Cup pedigree highlighted by that win over Leeds, and that mood was vividly illustrated by the programme cover for Hunslet's visit, which centred on a photograph of Murphy in action in that epic of fourteen years earlier. Leigh, who had won the championship under Murphy in 1981/82, were struggling somewhat in the league and would, indeed, be relegated at the end of the season. Nevertheless, they were fancied to overcome a Hunslet outfit also destined to go down, particularly as adverse weather caused the tie to be postponed on its scheduled date and rearranged for a cold Wednesday evening.

Home supporters could, in the circumstances, be forgiven at half-time if they set about preparing for a home quarter-final tie with Hull KR. Their favourites, after all, had gone in at the break 22-4 ahead against a hapless Hunslet side that had barely got going. Murphy, ever concerned for his fellow coaches, commiserated with visiting coach Paul Daley as the teams trooped off, tweaking Daley's cheek and saying, 'hard lines, son.' The legend had every reason for confidence. Hunslet, who had rarely threatened in the opening period, had been limited to a couple of penalties by winger Eric Fitzsimons and the conversation among away supporters (or at least two of them) turned to whether a visit to the pub would be more attractive than seeing out the second half.

Daley, however, was renowned for the power of his half-time pep talks and, perhaps motivated by Murphy, he outshone himself in the bid to inspire his players. None of this, of course, had been in the province of the supporters who, having expected more from a side that had travelled across the Pennines on the back of four successive wins, settled back to see the game out. An early try by powerful prop Andy Bateman at least suggested that Hunslet were going to make some impression on the game, and Fitzsimons's conversion ensured the respectability of double figures. The mood, though, improved markedly when Australian second row Mal Graham powered over, Fitzsimons again improving, and a touchdown to packman Andy Marson raised Hunslet's small band of supporters to a frenzy. Suddenly, incredibly, the tie had been transformed. And the momentum

Leigh 27   Hunslet 28

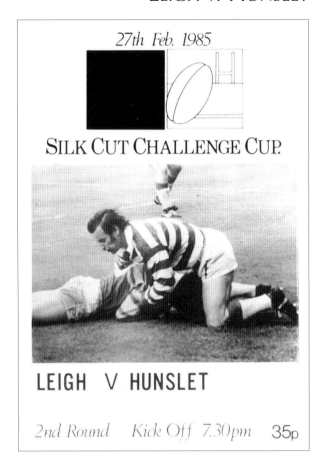

27th Feb. 1985

SILK CUT CHALLENGE CUP.

LEIGH V HUNSLET

2nd Round   Kick Off 7.30pm   35p

Alex Murphy had enjoyed the upper hand, as player-coach, when his side disposed of Leeds in the 1971 Challenge Cup final and Leigh had no hesitation in reminding Hunslet of the fact, reproducing an action shot of the event for their programme cover when the Elland Road men travelled to Lancashire for the midweek cup tie fourteen years later. There was, though, to be no joy this time for the Hilton Park outfit.

generated by the rally was becoming unstoppable. Fitzsimons' fifth goal had reduced the deficit to a single point, Leigh having kept themselves in front with a John Woods drop goal, but Hunslet were not going to be denied.

Leigh, who had opened with two Steve Davies tries and touchdowns for Phil Fox, Graham Worgan and John Henderson, with Woods kicking a goal, stretched their lead with Fox's second score, but scrum half Graham King scampered over as time began to run out, Fitzsimons again improving to secure, astonishingly, a lucrative home quarter-final tie with the side they had beaten two years earlier, Hull KR.

An incredible fightback was rightly celebrated in style by the players and also by Daley who, on leaving the playing area, gave Alex Murphy suitable solace by approaching him, tweaking his cheek and commiserating, 'hard lines, Dad!'

Leigh: C. Johnson, Worgan, Henderson, Davies, Fox, Woods, P. Johnson, Pyke, Tabern, Van Bellen, Clarke, Cottrell, Thomas. Subs: Stephens, Ainsworth or Howarth.

Hunslet: Kay, Hullock, Tate, Roe, Fitzsimons, Cawood, King, Byron, Gray, Bateman, Graham, Idle, Wolford. Subs: Murray, Bowden or Rudd.

WIGAN v. HUNSLET

Date: 14 April 1985   **Division One**
Location: Central Park, Wigan   **Referee:** Mr J.T. Kendrew (Castleford)

Wigan, only a month away from winning the Challenge Cup with the 28-24 verdict in the Wembley classic with Hull, experienced the other side of the sporting coin as cobbled-together Hunslet, with a trialist on the left wing and young second row Billy Bowden on the right flank, recorded an amazing victory. Hunslet, already doomed to relegation and with something of a patched-up side, turned the tables on the high-fliers after having allowed an early lead to be transformed into a 16-8 interval deficit.

The Elland Road outfit, with only one previous away win in league competition that season (at Workington, 9-6, in late October) went into the game on the back of a seven-match losing run. High hopes of repeating their 1983 Challenge Cup success over Hull KR, when the Robins returned to Elland Road in the 1985 quarter-finals, had been dashed with a 27-7 defeat and the emphatic nature of that setback seemed to affect morale as Leeds, Oldham, Hull KR and Featherstone Rovers all topped the forty-point mark in league encounters. There were signs, however, that the tide was turning when Barrow were held to a 14-7 scoreline at Craven Park, followed by a 10-6 home defeat by Featherstone, and that improvement came to notable fruition at Central Park.

Wigan, after their epic 18-11 victory over Hull KR in the Challenge Cup semi-final at Elland Road, had themselves suffered a dip in form. A comfortable 28-2 home win over Oldham three days later was followed by successive defeats at the hands of Hull, Leeds, Bradford Northern and St Helens, before the slide was arrested with victories at Oldham and Widnes.

Hunslet, though, were to restore the furrows to the brows of the Pie Eaters. Australian second row Mal Graham, a man who made a huge impact in his time at Elland Road for his fearsome running and imposing defence, had arguably his best game for his adopted club. The Hunslet captain assisted in centre Paul Murray's first-half try, with stand-off Steve Diamond supplying the final pass and adding the goal, and went on to net a second-half brace of his own as the visitors bettered Wigan's fightback. Roy Sampson secured the majority of possession when brought on as hooker in the closing period, when Wigan missed injured number nine Nicky Kiss, who had been withdrawn in the fifty-second minute.

Wigan, in an echo of the 1959 Championship semi-final on the same ground, simply wilted under the pressure, with only half-backs Brett Kenny and Mike Ford, together with second row Brian Dunn, escaping criticism. Hunslet had rocked the home side when a ten-point lead was established with Murray's converted score, Diamond having kicked an earlier goal and subsequently adding his second penalty. But Wigan appeared to have woken up when New Zealand captain Graeme West, winger Dave Wood and Ford slipped over in a blistering eight-minute spell, winger Henderson Gill adding a couple of conversions to post a comfortable interval lead. Hunslet, however, were in total control in the second half. Sampson, introduced at half-time, showed vision and skill in

---

Wigan 16   Hunslet 19

Rampaging second-row forward Billy Bowden, drafted in on the wing, served Hunslet well in one of the surprise results of the season.

sending Graham over in the forty-fifth minute, Diamond improving. With Wigan struggling to keep tabs on speedy scrum half Graham King, the opportunity arose for Mal Graham to make use of the extra space and the second row helped restore Hunslet's lead when he powered over for a scintillating solo score on the hour. And that was how it stayed until the last minute, when Diamond fired a 35-yard drop goal to seal a memorable victory in which revenge was gained for the 48-16 home defeat in December.

The win, however, may have taken a great deal out of coach Paul Daley's men, who faced a sorely testing close to the campaign. Only three days later, Hunslet travelled to St Helens and were on the receiving end of a 68-7 hiding. And, the following Sunday, Wigan's Challenge Cup final opponents, Hull, brought the side's Division One odyssey to a close with a 58-26 imposition at the Boulevard. Hunslet, despite that heady afternoon at Central Park, had had a fairly miserable experience in the top flight in which nine defeats on the trot at the start of the campaign had set the platform for a sorry eight months. Defence, a notable feature of the win at Wigan, had been a perennial problem, notably in the 41-40 home defeat in early September at the hands of Barrow, who scored three late tries to post an incredible result.

Daley's men showed, with a run of six successive wins from mid-February to early March and culminating in an amazing Challenge Cup fightback at Leigh and a fine league win over Castleford, exactly what their capabilities were. And they were again revealed, emphatically, and not for the first time, at Central Park.

Wigan: Edwards, Wood, Whitfield, Donlan, Gill, Kenny, Ford, Courtney, Kiss, Campbell, West, Dunn, Scott. Sub: Du Toit.

Hunslet: Kay, Bowden, Murray, Evans, Diamond, King, Van Bellen, Gray, Marson, Graham, Idle, Mitchell. Subs: Hughes, Sampson.

Hunslet v. Swinton

Date: 17 May 1987

Location: Old Trafford, Manchester

Division Two Premiership final

Referee: Mr J. McDonald (Wigan)

The concept of a Premiership 'double-header' at Old Trafford, with supporters getting two matches for the price of one, was among British rugby league's more successful innovations during a period of surefootedness by the sport's hierarchy. The previous highest attendance for the Premiership final, which had been introduced in 1974/75 as an end-of-season knockout competition to replace the old championship play-offs, had been the 29,448 that turned up for the clash of Hull and Hull KR at Headingley in 1981. Other than on that occasion, the crowd had never topped 20,000. By contrast, an attendance of 38,756 amassed at Manchester United's ground for the first of what was to become one of the most popular events in the rugby league calendar until the introduction of Super League in 1996.

Hunslet, as Division Two champions, could have been viewed as favourites although the two meetings between the sides that season gave no hint of supremacy either way. Swinton had been beaten 12-4 at home, while the Lions had won the return at Station Road 14-12. The final table confirmed Hunslet in pole position, with 25 victories from their 28 games. Coaches David Ward and Peter Jarvis had moulded a team that was thoroughly focussed under skipper Webb, with Platt an outstanding ball-handler in the second row.

Hunslet, however, lacking injured skipper Terry Webb at Old Trafford, switched fellow Aussie Graeme Jennings from hooker. Jennings, ironically, had no need to swap jerseys. Webb, originally selected at hooker at the beginning of the season, had cut the sleeves short; and had been compelled by Ward to wear that shirt thereafter as punishment. The captain, despite his lack of respect for shirtsleeves, had plenty to offer; including superb organising abilities, a rock-solid defence and a mental and physical toughness that was going to be missed. The speedy Chris 'Billy' Bowden was called into the second row in his absence, Phil Gibson stepping in at hooker. Hunslet abjured the proven successful gambit of bringing on Bowden for the final quarter to replace prop Keith Mason who, on this occasion, started on the bench with Andy Sykes on from the start. Meanwhile, the backs were hit by injury to winger Mick Bell. Phil Tate and Warren Wilson took the outside berths while regular centre Gary Senior was named as a substitute, his spot going to Colin Penola.

With the build-up far from ideal it was hardly surprising that Hunslet, who had beaten Carlisle 54-0 and Rochdale Hornets 32-8 on the way to Old Trafford, came off second best as they featured in their biggest game since the 1965 Yorkshire Cup final. Swinton, who had accounted for Bramley (59-14) and Whitehaven (12-6), owed much to a dominant front row of Joe Grima, Roby Muller and hooker Gary Ainsworth, who collected the Man of the Match award in recognition of having been involved in four of his side's five tries, and his 11-4 dominance in the scrums. Ainsworth, however – who was helped in his bid by the departure on the half hour of Gibson – was pushed as the game's

---

Hunslet 10   Swinton 27

Speedy scrum half Graham King, a prolific try scorer, was a key figure for Hunslet throughout much of the 1980s.

top player by his loose forward Les Holliday. But Swinton also owed their victory to two slices of good fortune, each involving an Old Trafford upright.

Hunslet were just one point adrift at 5-4 down as the last minute of the first half ticked away, when Les Holliday attempted to land his second drop goal. His shot rebounded off a post into the arms of Swinton second row Alan Derbyshire who raced over for a shock try. Doubts over whether Derbyshire had been onside were brushed aside on the basis that the ball had touched a Hunslet player en route to the posts. Winger Andy Rippon added the easy conversion to leave Hunslet shaken at seven points down. And the south Leeds outfit's mood was not helped at the close of the game when Swinton staged an incredible repeat, scrum half Martin Lee gathering on this occasion before sending Ainsworth over for another converted try.

Although those two freak scores helped the Lions to a flattering scoreline, few in the Hunslet camp were inclined to quibble over Swinton's right to the Premiership Trophy, particularly as the Manchester club had been obliged to overcome its own troubles, including the loss of centre Paul Topping (fractured cheekbone) and Alan Ratcliffe (broken leg) in the twenty-fifth and sixty-sixth minutes respectively. Disappointing Hunslet, who had free scoring scrum half Graham King kept under wraps, were well served by explosive prop Andy Bateman, who crashed over for each of his side's tries. Bateman's first, in the eighteenth minute and courtesy of a well-timed pass by second row Alan Platt, levelled matters after winger Derek Bate had crossed for Swinton, but his second touchdown wasn't enough to keep Hunslet in serious contention in the last forty minutes. The Lions eased clear with tries by Grima and Lee, while Rippon totalled three goals.

Hunslet, however, despite missing out on the £4,000 winners' cheque, had the satisfaction of having secured the major prize of the championship and a £1,500 runners-up prize.

Hunslet: Kay, Tate, Penola, Irvine, Wilson, Coates, King, Sykes, Gibson, Bateman, Platt, Bowden, Jennings. Subs: Senior, Mason.

Swinton: Viller, Bate, Topping, Brown, Rippon, Snape, Lee, Grima, Ainsworth, Muller, Derbyshire, L. Holliday, M. Holliday. Subs: Allen, Ratcliffe.

HUNSLET v. SALFORD

Date: 12 February 1995   **Challenge Cup fourth round**
Location: McLaren Field, Bramley   **Referee:** Mr I. Ollerton (Wigan)

Hunslet, ensconced in the lower half of Division Two, staged an impressive recovery to force a draw with Division One opponents who perhaps contributed to their own downfall in the immediate build-up to the game. Salford arrived at McLaren Field, Bramley – where Hunslet were playing after having been persuaded to leave Elland Road because of the forthcoming European soccer championships – with a number of players apparently hungry. Whether it was that, or sheer greed, or even the impossibly tempting aroma emanating from the ground's fast-food stall, several spectators insisted that they had spotted a number of Red Devils tucking into beefburgers and hot dogs when perhaps they should have been loosening up on the pitch.

The visitors' coach Gary Jack, the former Australian Test full-back, would have been aware that his opponents were going into the game with four successive victories behind them. Hunslet had crushed Highfield 56-0 in mid-January, when right-winger Scott Limb set a new record in the post-1973 era with five tries, and that success had been followed by a 64-4 demolition of amateurs Wigan St Patricks in the third round of the Challenge Cup. Coach Steve Ferres had subsequently steered his side to a 32-12 league win at one of his former clubs, Carlisle, and that success had been followed by a 25-18 home victory over Rochdale Hornets. Hunslet, therefore, despite their comparatively lowly status, were a side in form.

Salford, who had lost three successive games up to and including the New Year's Day clash at Bradford, had subsequently narrowly beaten Sheffield Eagles and Halifax, with a 34-0 defeat at Workington between those games suggesting that the Red Devils could perhaps be susceptible to collapse. That was precisely what Salford did in the final quarter of a rousing tie. Stand-off Steve Blakeley, one of the few Reds to emerge with any real credit, appeared to have booked his side's place in the fifth round when he crossed in the sixty-second minute and added the conversion. His goal gave the visitors the cushion of a sixteen-point lead and the majority of the 1,112 spectators reckoned that the match was over bar the shouting. Not, however, Hunslet, as Salford visibly withered in the face of a stunning onslaught and, perhaps, through the effects of their pre-match snack.

Second row Mick Coyle set the agenda with a sensational solo try, registered after a storming diagonal run through the Red Devils' defence, and that score was followed by a short-range effort by substitute Neil Lee. Prop Richard Pell converted Lee's touchdown to reduce the arrears to six points. And, with Hunslet in the ascendancy, a quick tap penalty and burst by bustling stand-off David Brook led to centre Giles Boothroyd sending scrum half David Close over the whitewash. Pell, who had missed three previous attempts, kept his nerve to land the conversion that squared matters and force the replay that Ferres' charges deserved.

Hunslet, indeed, had been the better side in the early stages. Pell had crossed in the first minute and the only real resistance to the home bid in the opening quarter came from Blakeley and hard-

---

Hunslet 32   Salford 32

Mick Coyle, one of Hunslet's finest servants, is hauled down short of the try line by Salford's scrambling defence, with full-back Eric Kibe in support. Prop Steve Pryce – like Coyle, another man to give the club great service – is in the background.

working second row Bob Marsden. Salford took the lead when full-back Gary Tyrer and hooker Jonathan Quigley nipped over before the half hour, Hunslet responding in the meantime with a classically worked try for Close, who popped up on the end of an incisive move sparked by hooker Chris Watson and continued by Coyle and Brook. Pell landed his second goal of the half to nose the home side in front but the fine work was undone when, with the interval approaching, an ambitious pass by loose forward Matt Lambert was intercepted by Salford centre Martin Birkett who duly sent Great Britain winger Phil Ford in at the corner. Matters got worse for Hunslet. Within ten minutes of the resumption Salford had netted two further tries, Marsden ploughing over from fifteen yards and Ford crossing to forge a fourteen-point lead. Boothroyd nipped over in response but a piece of ill-fortune, when a Salford pass was knocked down by a home player to present Blakeley with his simple try, seemed to have clinched an away win.

That wasn't to be, courtesy of Hunslet's inspiring rally that echoed the Challenge Cup win against the same opponents in 1946. There was, however, to be no reward in the replay. Salford, perhaps with Garry Jack monitoring a few diets, eased to a 52-10 victory at the Willows, losing at home to Featherstone Rovers in the next round. Hunslet, meanwhile, won seven of their last ten league games to suggest that the following season, when the club would return 'home' to a new ground adjacent to the Parkside of beloved memory, could be one in which fortunes would at last take a sustained upturn.

Hunslet: Kibe, Limb, Farrell, Boothroyd, White, Brook, Close, Pell, Watson, Pryce, Jowitt, Coyle, Lambert.
   Subs: Stott, Lee.
Salford: Tyrer, McAvoy, Panapa, Birkett, Ford, Blakeley, Lee, Young, Quigley, Eccles, Marsden, Randall, Blease.
   Subs: Critchley, Webster.

Hunslet Hawks v. Leigh Centurions

Date: 19 November 1995

Location: South Leeds Stadium

Stones Centenary Championship Division Two

Referee: Mr G. Owram (Bradford)

After twenty-two years away, nomadic Hunslet returned to their spiritual home to a resounding reception from a packed house that included many former Parkside greats.

The Hawks had hoped to be able to open the season at their new ground with the home game against York, who had provided the last opposition at Parkside back in 1973 – Hunslet, in a neat twist, were the last visitors to Wiggington Road in 1989 – but delays in completing the South Leeds Stadium had resulted in those plans being shelved. Leigh, however, were compliant guests, losing comfortably after early resistance to help with the celebrations.

The teams entered the pitch between a guard of honour comprising former players and all the heroes, on taking their seats in the stand, were able to contemplate the scene of their former glories simply by glancing to their left, where the site of the old Parkside ground was marked by the poplar trees that had formed the boundary to the cricket field. Many of those ex-players, together with the current players and the Hunslet supporters in the close-to-capacity 2,350 crowd, would have taken in a deep breath in an effort to draw on the spirit of the past, and that approach certainly galvanised the Hawks' team. The author of this book, in his report for the *Rugby Leaguer*, reported: 'There were tears before and after the game yesterday as Hunslet made an emotional return home after a generation's absence.

'Many of the great and the good from Hunslet's past were paraded before the crowd prior to kick-off, led by Sam Newbound of the 1938 Championship side, with his captain, the matchless Jack Walkington, bringing up the rear. And in the middle, among a host of other greats, were most of the 1965 Wembley side.

'The new stadium looked magnificent under the floodlights as the evening drew in, with the city of Leeds providing a beautiful backdrop under the night sky and the chugging steam train on Middleton Railway – the oldest in the world – adding a further sense of history.

'Amid all this Hunslet put on a special show for the fans, despite losing their way a little around half-time.

'Superbly marshalled by Lee Hanlan, a local lad on loan from Wakefield until the end of the season, the Hawks recovered from an uncertain start to shoot into a 17-2 lead by the half hour.

'The party spirit then seemed to get to the players – and enthusiastic Leigh, not prepared to play the fall guys, recovered to go in only 17-10 down at half-time.

'The Centurions' impressive stand-off Chris Wilkinson had put his side ahead with a fourth-minute penalty to earn his place in the record books, before Hunslet drew level with a David Close goal.

'With Hanlan bossing the show Hunslet began to dominate – and when he and Giles Boothroyd combined to free Gary Richardson, the winger surged through from forty yards, leaving full-back Glyn Davies sprawling, to touch down in the thirteenth minute.

Hunslet Hawks 37   Leigh Centurions 10

Hunslet Hawks v. Leigh Centurions

Coming home. Former Hunslet players create a guard of honour as captain Giles Boothroyd leads the Hawks onto the South Leeds Stadium pitch for the first time.

'Close couldn't convert but Hanlan dropped a goal six minutes later; and after Mick Coyle had been held on his back, Steve Pryce crashed over off Hanlan's pass, Close goaling to stretch the Hawks' lead.

'When Richardson again powered over, on the half hour, a fairy tale romp looked likely. But as Hunslet relaxed, Leigh bounced back, Wilkinson setting up the position for John Perigo to send Tau Liku over. And, on the stroke of half-time, Robinson crossed off a Davies pass but, fortunately for the Hawks and for the script, Wilkinson failed with both conversion attempts.

'A further score to the visitors shortly after half-time could well have led to a Leigh win but the Centurions were the perfect guests on this great south Leeds occasion, and Hunslet steadied following coach Steve Ferres' forceful pep talk.

'After having soaked Leigh pressure, Coyle had his second disallowed "try" of the afternoon when he was brought back for a forward pass. But Hunslet got the break they needed when Liku was caught offside in the fifty-eighth minute to give Close a simple goal.

'Two minutes later, Close and Tim Sharp combined for Richard Baker to send Jason Viller and give Hunslet a handy cushion.

'It wasn't needed. Eight minutes from time another excellent Baker pass put Viller through for his second score; four minutes later substitute Bob Grant scorched over from thirty yards, and on the stroke of time Baker bagged a superb score of his own when he kicked through and outpaced and outwitted the Leigh defence.

'The hooter sounded to resounding cheers from the Hunslet faithful who had celebrated the occasion with a rendition of *We've Swept the Seas before Boys*.

'Will those great days of the likes of the Terrible Six, of Albert Goldthorpe, Billy Batten, Jack Walkington, Geoff Gunney and Brian Gabbitas return?

'It's impossible to say. But, back home at last, Hunslet now at least have the chance.'

Hunslet Hawks: Baker, White, Viller, Boothroyd, Richardson, Hanlan, Close, Lambert, Brook, Pryce, Coyle, Levien, Sharp.

Leigh Centurions: Davies, Sarsfield, Hadcroft, O'Loughlin, Cheetham, Wilkinson, Robinson, Liku, Bannister, Perigo, Wilson, McGughan, Jukes. Burgess, Grainey.

WIDNES VIKINGS v. HUNSLET HAWKS

Date: 23 March 1997

Location: Naughton Park, Widnes

Silk Cut Plate semi-final

Referee: Mr S. Presley (Castleford)

Hunslet booked a return to Wembley after a thirty-two year gap with an unexpected but thoroughly deserved victory over Doug Laughton's fancied Widnes side. The fact that the Hawks would not be appearing in the main event – the Challenge Cup final – but in the inaugural Plate decider, contested by teams knocked out in the first round of the Challenge Cup, failed to curb the delight of hard-working chairman Grahame Liles, his equally committed wife Margaret, or their fellow directors. Hunslet, for the Liles family and their loyal core of supporters, were back in the limelight and the success under ambitious young coach David Plange vindicated the decision to move from Leeds United's Elland Road ground to the South Leeds Stadium only eighteen months previously.

There was added piquancy, too, in the fact that Hunslet's victims in the semi-final, Widnes, had also been their opponents on the first occasion that the then-Parksiders had appeared at Wembley, in 1934. Hunslet had been fairly clear-cut winners, by 11-5, on that occasion but it was far more tense sixty-three years later. The Hawks were grateful for a couple of tactical gaffes by Widnes that helped Plange renew acquaintance with Hull KR, one of his former sides as a powerhouse winger, in the final. In particular, the Vikings were to regret the decision to spurn a couple of drop goal attempts in the closing seconds that could have secured extra time. Widnes also opted to run the ball early in the second period when a simple penalty was on offer, prop Ian Connor losing the ball on the first tackle.

Regardless of those errors, Hunslet fully merited their success. Australian stand-off Paul Mansson, who had celebrated his twenty-fifth birthday earlier in the week, had extra cause for cheer with a superlative match-winning performance that was the difference between the two sides. Mansson scored Hunslet's first try, a trademark seventy-five-metre scorcher as half-time approached after he had intercepted a speculative pass by Vikings centre Peter Smith. It was also the stand-off who sparked the Hawks' second score. His pinpoint chip kick – early, as on previous occasions, in the tackle count – gave full-back Chris Ross the chance to pounce for a score that stretched Hunslet's lead to seven points.

Widnes, who had opened with a try in the fourth minute by second row Gareth Cunningham, goaled by stand-off Paul Gartland, prevented the Hawks from extending their lead when Smith pulled off a try-saving tackle on Paul White. The Vikings clawed their way back into contention with a touchdown for New Zealand centre Boycie Nelson, who nipped over from a Phil Kendrick pass, Gartland adding the difficult goal. Hunslet restored their advantage when second row Craig Booth popped up on the end of an incisive raid involving scrum half David Brook and loose forward Gareth Cochrane, Booth adding his third goal of the game. But Widnes refused to lie down, mounting a late attack that led to Kendrick crossing three minutes from the close, substitute Ben Lythe adding the extras. Time, though, was on Hunslet's side.

There was less joy for the Hawks in the final. The event was marred by a bomb scare that delayed the kick-off and Hunslet, who had beaten Hull KR in the last major final between the sides – the

---

Widnes Vikings 18   Hunslet Hawks 19

Hawks full-back Chris Ross is congratulated by Paul Mansson and the rest of the Hunslet side after beating the Widnes defence to Mansson's telling kick.

1962 Yorkshire Cup decider – were heavily beaten by a Robins outfit in which stand-off Stanley Gene excelled. Mansson, playing behind a beaten pack, was unable to display his undoubted skills on the most major of stages, despite a fine start in which hooker Graham Southernwood burrowed over after only four minutes. Rovers hit back with touchdowns by centre Rob D'Arcy and second row Paul Fletcher, full-back Mike Fletcher adding a goal, but the Hawks were on level terms by the half-hour mark, Mansson having scored a brilliant forty-metre solo try and loose forward Craig Booth landing a penalty. Hull KR, though, assumed control by the interval with converted tries by winger Jon Adams and stand-off Gary Atkins. Gene forced his way over a minute after the restart and Atkins went in for his second try before the Hawks renewed acquaintance with the scoreboard with a touchdown by centre Mike Pechey.

The rest of the game, however, belonged to the Robins, who made certain of the Plate and the £50,000 winners' cheque (£10,000 more than Challenge Cup runners-up Bradford received) with two more tries for Gene, further touchdowns to Adams and Paul Fletcher, and a late effort by loose forward Chris Charles. Mike Fletcher, who would later join the Hawks, totalled eight goals. Hunslet, however, had again appeared on the major stage. And there was no small consolation in the £30,000 runners-up cheque.

Widnes Vikings: Broadbent, Thorniley, Nelson, Kendrick, Smith, Gartland, Waring, Connor, Donno, Hansen, Cunningham, Myler, Cassidy. Subs: Bloom, Collier, Lythe, Hunter.

Hunslet Hawks: Ross, Baker, Coult, Boothroyd, Plange, Mansson, Brook, Rushton, Southernwood, Tuffs, Booth, Flowers, Cochrane. Subs: Paul White, Coyle, Pryce, Phil White.

Dewsbury Rams v. Hunslet Hawks

Date: 25 September 1999

Location: Headingley, Leeds

Northern Ford Premiership grand final

Referee: Mr S. Ganson (St Helens)

To the victor the spoils, goes the old adage.

Not, however, in professional rugby league in the closing stages of the twentieth century. Both sides went into the game bidding for the title of Northern Ford Premiership champions but aware that the main prize of promotion to Super League was another matter altogether. The deliberations of the Independent Franchise Panel – a group of four or five unnamed people charged with the task of vetting Super League applications – were of rather more importance than anything that happened on the pitch. The plans of directors, the strategies of coaches, the hard work of volunteers; all were of less validity than considerations on whether the side that prevailed in the NFP grand final fitted a raft of criteria including the suitability of its ground. To the chagrin of the likes of Hunslet and Dewsbury, the fact that many – in fact the majority – of clubs already in Super League fell short on a number of points was not deemed to be a relevant factor in submissions by clubs on the outside. The feeling, therefore, was that whoever won at Headingley would face more than a few subsequent problems; and so it proved.

A drop goal midway through the second half by Hawks second row Jamie Leighton turned out to be the match-winning closing score of a pulsating final. Leighton's one-pointer, however, far from bringing joy and hope to the sporting public of south Leeds, set Hunslet on a path to decline. The portents were ominous even before the post-match celebrations were over. Whereas, thirty-four years earlier, Hunslet coach Fred Ward and his chairman Harold Inman had received congratulatory telegrams from their counterparts at Leeds United before leaving the changing rooms, on this occasion the immediate feedback was loud whispers in the Headingley tea room to the effect that the Hawks' hopes of inclusion in the top flight were non-existent.

The whisperers were well-informed. With Leeds City Council reneging on a promised upgrade of the South Leeds Stadium – a pledge that had persuaded Hunslet to move out of Elland Road to help accommodate the European soccer championships – the responsibility fell on the RFL to stand by one of its older and more famous clubs. Hunslet supporters would say that the RFL failed in the task.

Proposals by Hunslet to stage the bigger games, against the likes of Bradford Bulls and Leeds Rhinos, at other venues were brushed aside, and the possibility of playing at the Jungle was turned down on the basis that Castleford's ground was 'not fit for Super League'. Featherstone Rovers' Post Office Road was vetoed as being a few seats short, and that ruling was also made when the Hawks considered – fancifully – Scunthorpe's ground. The consequence was that Hunslet had to release many of the players who had, in terms of the action on the pitch, earned a place in the top flight. Crowds inevitably dwindled and the Hawks plunged into a downwards spiral.

Hunslet director Bill Fotherby, who had been a key figure in restoring Leeds United to the top of the soccer world, subsequently resigned, thoroughly disillusioned. In the immediate aftermath of the

---

Dewsbury Rams 11   Hunslet Hawks 12

DEWSBURY RAMS v. HUNSLET HAWKS

The Hunslet squad celebrates after earning a return to the top flight. The laughter was to turn to tears when a place in Super League was denied the Hawks by the Rugby Football League.

win he had insisted: 'The people at Super League must not ignore us. If they take away the incentive of promotion they will kill the game.

'Some people say there shouldn't be two Super League teams in Leeds but that's nonsense. It's a big city and can easily accommodate two teams. The people of south Leeds and the players deserve promotion, they've earned it and I'm going to do my best to make sure they get it.'

Fotherby's plans for terraces on the railway side of the ground, however, failed to come to fruition for want of funding and council support, leaving the players in particular an abject and frustrated bunch.

Dewsbury had opened the scoring with a drop goal by stand-off Richard Agar, a penalty by scrum half Barry Eaton and a try for winger Adrian Flynn. Hunslet were level by the break, right centre Paul Cook crossing, Chris Ross adding the extras and scrum half Latham Tawhai firing a drop goal before left centre John Higgins got the Hawks in front with a try shortly after the restart. Loose forward Damian Ball replied for the Rams but Eaton's missed conversion attempt left the sides level until Leighton's match winner.

Hunslet duly held out for a result that may be the only instance in sport of winners turning out to be losers – a poor reward for players of whom Fotherby enthused: 'The players are a different class. What other players would give up their bonuses to pay for their own hotel when we played up at Whitehaven? Certainly no footballer I've ever met.'

Dewsbury Rams: Graham, Godfrey, Evans, O'Meara, Flynn, Agar, Eaton, Boothroyd, Delaney, Long, Spink, Haigh, Ball. Subs: Williams, Richardson, Hicks, Medley.

Hunslet Hawks: Fatnowna, Ross, Irwin, Cook, Higgins, Vassilakopoulos, Tawhai, Hayes, Pachniuk, Pryce, Wilson, Leighton, St Hilaire. Subs: Coyle, Kennedy, Thackray, Baker.

Hunslet Hawks v. Huddersfield Giants

Date: 9 February 2003

Location: South Leeds Stadium

Powergen Challenge Cup fourth round

Referee: Mr S. Presley (Castleford)

Huddersfield Giants, newly promoted to the Tetley's Super League, travelled to National League Two underdogs Hunslet as red-hot favourites to progress in the 2003 Powergen Challenge Cup. The Giants went into the game chasing a new British record of thirty successive victories and, with coach Tony Smith at the helm, were hopeful of not only making an impact on the Silk Cut Challenge Cup but of also consolidating their status in the top flight after having suffered relegation the previous season.

Hunslet, by contrast, were still feeling the effects of having been denied entry to Super League four years earlier. The Hawks, now in the bottom tier, had lost coach David Plange to Warrington and were steadily rebuilding, with committed local talent, under Roy Sampson. His side had already posted something of an upset in the competition, having disposed of French outfit Pia at the South Leeds Stadium in the preceding round. Pia, lying third in the French league, were far from pushovers and had boasted in their squad three Australian players with State of Origin experience. However, the Hawks, despite going behind to an early try by stand-off Adam Nable, had dominated much of the game, inspirational loose forward Gareth Naylor closing with a hat-trick. Second row Danny Fearon had also crossed, courtesy of an outrageous dummy, and winger George Raynor clinched the success with a late touchdown that settled Hunslet's nerves after the sin-binning of Mick Coyle and the departure with cartilage and ligament damage of influential stand-off Andy Bastow, who was consequently ruled out of the Huddersfield tie.

Sampson, a player of monumental spirit in his day, had obviously instilled in his charges the belief that victory was far from an impossible dream. And, in one of the major upsets in Challenge Cup history, his players turned his vision into reality with an even more imposing success against the Giants. There was a feeling on the press bench prior to kick-off that although Huddersfield were certainly capable of cantering through the tie there was a possibility of an upset if Hunslet could play to their maximum potential and if Huddersfield slipped below their best. The latter proved to be the case in a match that evoked memories of the Challenge Cup success over Hull KR exactly twenty years earlier. Huddersfield failed to overcome the absence, through injury, of influential stand-off Stanley Gene and loose forward Steve McNamara. The Giants, however, didn't appear to have any problems when Australian stand-off Brandon Costin raced over in the very first minute, courtesy of a break and well-timed pass by second row Jim Gannon.

Although Costin sliced his conversion attempt wide, Huddersfield continued to press and seemed likely to add to their opening score. Hunslet, however, hit back against the run of play, full-back Richard Baker racing into the line from a scrum in front of his own posts to free centre Iain Higgins, who held off the cover in a chase to halfway before sending speedy winger Bryn Powell, the former Hunslet Warrior and BARLA Great Britain Under-23 international, over from fifty metres. Stand-off

Hunslet Hawks 18

Huddersfield Giants 14

HUNSLET HAWKS v. HUDDERSFIELD GIANTS

Johnny Liddell couldn't convert from near the touchline and Hunslet were again put on the back foot when, in a rare piece of quality action, Giants hooker Paul March flighted a long ball for winger Marcus St Hilaire to race in at the corner.

The Hawks, however, with young ginger-haired prop Craig Ibbetson in inspired form, reproduced the spirit shown in the third round victory over French high-flyers Pia, bouncing back to take a grip on the tie with two tries in the space of three minutes. Second row Fearon, playing arguably his best game for Hunslet, was involved in both. The former Keighley packman set up the first with a blockbusting run, finished with a neat pass from which substitute forward Jon-Lee Lockwood charged over unopposed. And Hunslet were able to enjoy an eight-point lead at half-time when hooker Naylor and Fearon linked to send former Heworth prop Dan Briggs through, Liddell adding his second conversion in quick succession.

Huddersfield badly needed to net the opening score of the second half if they were to remain in contention, and the Giants got it when pacey Hawks scrum half Phil Hasty was unable to pull off an interception in his own twenty-metre area. The Giants scored directly from the scrum, Costin netting his second touchdown of the afternoon off a ball from loose forward Jarrod O'Doherty. Costin's conversion reduced the deficit to just two points and, with a quarter of the game remaining, the Super League outfit had reassumed the mantle of favourites. The young Hunslet team, however, displayed remarkable resolve that, aided by a severe attack of the 'dropsies' throughout the Huddersfield side, secured a shock.

Sampson's side had an escape when Giants prop Mick Slicker was held on his back over the home try-line, but that proved to be Huddersfield's last real opportunity to rescue the situation. With eleven minutes remaining, Giants substitute Ian Morrison conceded a penalty on his own twenty-metre line for holding down at the play-the-ball. Liddell took his time, kept his composure and fired over the goal that extended the lead to four points. Sustained pressure came to nothing for the hot favourites, despite a scare or two when possession was spilled deep in the home half, and Hunslet players and their loyal ban of supporters went wild at the final hooter. Smith, who twenty months later would guide Leeds Rhinos to the Tetley's Super League title and their first championship in thirty-two years, was typically magnanimous in defeat. He said: 'Hunslet's performance was a fine example of the romance of the Challenge Cup. We worked hard on not underestimating them but maybe some of my players did. Nobody died; we lost a football game, and the day belongs to Hunslet.'

Enthused Sampson: 'We are a confident team this year. When you win in the Challenge Cup, particularly the way we did today, you do get excited and you start to dream about who you will get in the next round. But in the end it doesn't make any difference. It's how you play, not who you play, that counts.'

Up to a point. Hunslet drew mighty Bradford Bulls in the fifth round. The tie was switched to Headingley in pursuit of a bigger gate, the South Leeds Stadium's capacity of 2,500 being deemed inadequate. Although the initiative paid off financially the Hawks went down to the heaviest defeat in the club's 120-year history, the players trooping off at the end to an 82-0 scoreline and a standing ovation.

Hunslet Hawks: Baker, Powell, Higgins, McGibbon, Raynor, Liddell, Hasty, Ibbetson, Naylor, Coyle, Wayne Freeman, Fearon, Seal. Subs: Brain, Hawley, Lockwood, Briggs.

Huddersfield Giants: Cooper, O'Hare, Bailey, Calland, St Hilaire, Costin, White, Slicker, March, Fleary, Crabtree, Gannon, O'Doherty. Subs: Whitaker, Turner, Wittenberg, Morrison.

Other titles published by Tempus

Hunslet Rugby League Club 1883-1973
LES HOOLE

This collection of over 200 images illustrates the history of Hunslet Rugby League Club, once one of the biggest names in the sport. It includes pictures from the record-breaking 'All Four Cups' campaign of 1907/08, the All Leeds Final of 1938 and other derby days as well as many of the other memorable moments in the Parksiders' history. An essential read for anyone with an interest in the club.

0 7524 1641 3

Yorkshire County Cricket Club 100 Greats
MICK POPE & PAUL DYSON

This book features 100 of the cricketers who have shaped Yorkshire CCC. From George Anderson, who first played for Yorkshire in 1850 – before the official club was constituted – through to Matthew Hoggard, who received his county cap in 2000, there have been many wonderful players, including the likes of Boycott, Trueman and Rhodes. Featuring biographies, statistics and illustrations, this is essential reading for all Tykes.

0 7524 2179 4

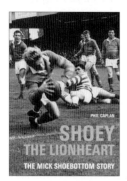

Shoey the Lionheart The Mick Shoebottom Story
PHIL CAPLAN

Mick Shoebottom was the ultimate player's player in the toughest of team sports. Hunslet-born, he was an integral part of the great Leeds side of the late 1960s and early 70s. Mick also played for his country and was a key member of the Great Britain side to win the Ashes in Australia in 1970. He went on two tours and won every domestic medal available until tragedy struck and he was grievously injured scoring perhaps the most infamous try witnessed at his beloved Headingley.

0 7524 3292 3

Leeds Legends
DAVID SAFFER

Hundreds of players have worn the shirt of Leeds United with pride over the decades. From loyal club stalwarts to controversial mavericks, many have attained legend status at Elland Road, and this book celebrates some of the men most prominent in the club's history. Over 100 great names are featured in *Leeds Legends*, including stars of the famous promotion, championship and cup winning sides. The book contains biographies, illustrations, statistics and a foreword by the late, great John Charles CBE.

0 7524 2700 8

If you are interested in purchasing other books published by Tempus, or in case you have difficulty finding any Tempus books in your local bookshop, you can also place orders directly through our website

www.tempus-publishing.com